OUR VAIKUṆṬHA PLANET

How to Eliminate Anxiety for 8 Billion People

Written by
Kāraṇodakaśāyī Viṣṇu Dāsa
Adhikārī
aka **Man Mohan Gupta**
M.A.(Oxon)

WOW Book Publishing™

First Edition Published by Man Mohan Gupta

Copyright date © December 2019 Man Mohan Gupta

WOW Book Publishing™

ISBN: 9781706686446

If you have any comments, questions or suggestions about this book, please do not hesitate to contact the author on:
101, Marley Walk, Willesden Green, London NW2 4PY, U.K.

Tel: +44 (0)20 8450 9603
Mobile: +44 (0)7913 897 406
Email: mohan.gupta108@yahoo.co.uk
Website: www.daivalimited.com
Facebook Name: Karanodakasayi Visnu Dasa Adhikari
Twitter: @Karanodakasayi
LinkedIn: Karanodakasayi Visnu Dasa Adhikari
Instagram: Karanodakasayi

Dedication

I would like to dedicate this book to my brother Raj, who has been by my side and a pillar of strength for me throughout my whole life. At 61 and 60 respectively, he has been through the many vicissitudes of life with me and, in particular, in shrinking my whole thinking from being grandiose over the years, to writing this book and making it a reality. Thank you, Raj; I love you!

Gratitude

If you ever get to write your own book, you will soon realise that publishing a book is never a one-man-affair and this is no exception. Apart from constant support from your family, in this case, my brother, Raj, for providing all the necessary provisions before you even put pen to paper, you will definitely need help from a publisher, even if you decide to self-publish.

In my case, it was Vishal Morjaria and his team at Wow Book Publishing that were the real driving force behind this book.

In particular, the indispensable help provided by my Book Angel, Pauline Barath in South Africa, who in liaising between publisher and author, made the book what it is today.

v

Further, you will also come to realise without someone to help you with your online presence, in this case, Hani Ali of Auxez Ltd., marketing your book will not be possible.

So, thank you Vishal, Pauline, Hani and also, Andrew Miller for watching over things as they developed. It is only when you have a team that anything is achieved in life. This then was my team.

Table of Contents

Testimonials

'Mohan holds an inner spirit of peace. He is caring and has a vision for peacefulness within communities. Mohan will tell you about this in his book, Our Vaikuṇṭha Planet: How to Eliminate Anxiety for 8 Billion People,

Andrew CM Miller
Award Winning Author,
& Transitional Coach

'You are a pure devotee.'

Srimati Kirti Ma Devi Dasi

'You are the most responsible person on the planet.'

His Holiness Om Visnupada Paramahamsa
Parivrajakacarya Astattora-sata
His Divine Grace Ksirodakasayi Visnu
Maharaja

OUR VAIKUNṬHA PLANET

'You are very nice.'

Sriman Caturbhuja Prabhu

'Get on with it.'

Sriman Sandipani Muni Prabhu

'You are a paramahamsa.'

Parama Advaiti Maharaja

'You are like a mad Avadhuta.'

Tribhuvanatha Prabhu

'You have the mace.'

Jagatbandhu Prabhu

'He will do everything.'

Srila Prabhupada

'It is simple and to the point.'

Asta-sakhi Devi Dasi on the book

About the Author

Karanodakasayi Visnu Dasa Adhikari, otherwise known as Man Mohan Gupta was born on 22nd February 1959 in Meerut, U.P., India and came to London, with his mother and brother when he was one year old in 1960, where he has had all his upbringing, including his schooling at St. Marylebone Grammar School and his further education at St. Catherine's College, Oxford.

He was initiated as a disciple of Om Visnupada Paramahamsa Parivrakajacarya Astottara–sata His Divine Grace A.C. Bhaktivedanta Svami Srila Prabhupada on 17th December 1969 at age ten at Bury Place, along with his father, mother and two brothers, and has worked for twelve public and private sector organisations in the U.K.

OUR VAIKUṆṬHA PLANET

Over the years he has advised the United Nations, Prime Ministers, Presidents and the Queen alike on matters of pressing interest and is looking to establish his own Institution, under the style of Daiva Varnasrama Dharma Institution, globally, beginning with the U.K. In line with the United Nations 17 Sustainable Development Goals, he is looking to create a Vaikuṇṭha planet out of this Earth planet by 1st January 2030.

Dear Reader

Thank you, ladies and gentlemen, for reading this book. It will change your life as it has changed mine. The subject matter is how we can all work together to create a Vaikuṇṭha Planet out of this beautiful Earth planet, and, in doing so, I hope to help 8 billion people overcome anxiety. That's definitely possible, provided we work towards achieving it.

We're travelling billions of miles in outer space to reach higher planets, and we've discovered the most wonderful technology to do that. So we can definitely discover the means to make everyone on this planet happy and contented, without anxiety. That is not a pipe dream; it is distinctly possible now. We simply have to gather the means and methods to do it. Some of the greatest teachers who have walked the earth have said so. They've said, "Praise the Lord with all thy heart and all thy soul, and one will come to know the glory of heaven on earth." For sure.

There's no doubt about it. Another great teacher has said *"bhaja govinda, bhaja govinda, bhaja govinda muda mate"*, meaning, *"Oh great fool, put down your weapons and ego and worship Govinda, worship Govinda, worship Govinda, the primeval Lord"*.

If you don't want to chant *"Hare Kṛṣṇa, Hare Kṛṣṇa, Kṛṣṇa Kṛṣṇa, Hare Hare, Hare Rāma, Hare Rāma, Rāma Rāma, Hare Hare"*, then you can chant the *"hallowed name of Jesus"*, or the *"beloved name of Allah, Jehovah, Yahweh, or Lord Buddha"*; it doesn't matter. Either way, we have to develop our love for God, for He is one without a second. And we are all worshiping that same one God, deriving the greatest of our benefits from Him.

Foreword

I have found Mohan to be an honest and simple soul, full of integrity, and rich in spirituality.

His book, *Our Vaikuṇṭha Planet: How to Eliminate Anxiety for 8 Billion People*, proves that not all paranoid schizophrenics are mad, a revelation for society and quite remarkable for its lucidity; it has the hallmarks of a real classic. Because of his high-level of self-knowledge and God-realisation, he may well turn out to be the Indian Einstein for whom the world is waiting.

Vishal Morjaria
Award Winning Author and
International Speaker

How to Read This Book

Please don't read this book without a pen in your hand. Go and get a pen straightaway, now! Whenever a thought comes whilst reading this book, jot it down immediately in the margins. You will then have a living, working, evolving book that will help you throughout your life.

With all the books I read, I like to underline things in red and make notes as I go along; in addition, I make it a point to read the book at least three times, in order to uncover its deepest lessons. I urge you to do the same.

In doing so, you will unpack some of the condensed wisdom that the book contains, and so, unwittingly, become the author of your own great book. By this, I wanted to demonstrate that a book is not just for passive reading; it is also a source of knowledge in which to write (library books being the exception of course!) and from which to develop positive characteristics.

The real joy will come when you actually practically implement what you have just read. Make a point of taking action straight-away when you read. This, then, is the art of studying.

9 Reasons Why You Should Read This Book

❖ **One:** *Brexit is coming around the corner, and we should know how to deal with it, irrespective of what happens further afield.*

There are trade wars going on with China and other things around the world. We have to see how we can deal with whatever is happening in the world, and rise above it.

❖ **Two:** *You can be sure there will be something else to worry about after Brexit, the trade wars, and everything else. So how do we deal with all that?*

❖ **Three:** *We can do that simply by learning to transcend the dualities of this world. We are in this world, but not of this world. Only then will we be in a safe boat.*

❖ **Four:** *Living in an atmosphere of non-anxiety is our normal, natural position.*

❖ **Five:** *Being free from anxiety allows us to think of the more important things in life - a life unexamined, is not worth living.*

❖ **Six:** *Let us see if we can finally get to know who we really are, where we have come from, and where are we going in the afterlife, having become free from anxiety from all this in the first place.*

❖ **Seven:** *Being anxious for food, shelter, clothing and all the basic necessities of life is to not realize that the good great Lord Almighty is taking care of all these things for millions and billions of living entities automatically like for the animals, birds, fishes,* *trees, plants, reptiles and insects and so on.*

❑ *They are all being taken care of by the Lord.*

❑ *7.1 Why won't He take care of me? He will, of course, and He does.*

❖ **Eight:** *All anxieties can be dealt with if we simply have faith in God. That's all.*

❖ **Nine:** *Dealing with anxiety also affects your work life and how you ultimately succeed in your work environment.*

Have you ever wondered how people can make a million pounds or billion pounds from doing what they most like doing? Yes: by following their passion in life and getting help from multi-millionaire programmes, which are to be found in practically any city in the world.

This is something I've been following myself in the last 18 months. I had a few things to say about that, which could help many people earn a living without having to have the drudgery of a 9 to 5 job.

I thought I'd give a little introduction to a new style of living through these programmes that only a very few number of people on the planet seem to know about. It seems not even 0.1% of the planet's population know how to make a good living from their current skillset.

You can find additional reading material, Videos and soon live streams about this on my website:

www.daivalimited.com

What is the Source of Anxiety?

Anxiety comes from not knowing what will happen to you in the future. If you have faith in the Lord, then you know your future is definitely bright. And all adversity that you meet in life is but to make you stronger.

A little germ injected during vaccination or inoculation helps the body fight off a bigger attack. This principle is used in homeopathy and in medicine in general.

Under the right care and treatment, there is no problem that cannot be solved with a positive mental attitude. It is how we receive so-called bad news that determines the outcome; not so much the bad news itself. Therefore, if we have a good philosophical, realistic outlook in life, then that's the battle almost half-won.

That's why constantly being in the association of good positive people who are always encouraging and giving yourself positive self-talk by chanting the maha-mantra, and always meditating on the good and the divine, can only accelerate your progress to a better future, and a better world.

These things are practical, and by patient determination, and a little enthusiastic endeavour, one can overcome whatever one may be worried about. The best way to overcome anxiety is to take action, and leave the result to Kṛṣṇa.

In my case, my action is to confide in anyone I can find around me. Within minutes, my problem is solved. It is having the faith to realize that the Lord speaks to you through people, or He gives a sign through a myriad of other ways, we just have to be alert to receiving them, and then we are always in peace.

Life might be a beast, but until you know how and why, you will still be suffering. So the question is, when will we learn our lesson? And will it be in time? These are the only points we have to consider.

Man Mohan Gupta

Everything is magic until we know how and why. Discover your purpose and fulfil it. The Lord's plan for us is always the best. Go with the flow of what the Lord wants us to do, and see the magic of life appear before your very eyes.

INTRODUCTION

The Birth of Our Vaikuṇṭha Planet

I first wanted to call this book, how I coped with anxiety, or how to cope with anxiety, as I was full of anxiety myself about how to write it, but then, as I began to manage myself better and set-to the task, I changed the title to **Our Vaikuṇṭha Planet**. I would like to start by how I came to write this book.

The first thing that comes to mind is a book I read by Julia Cameron back around the year 2006 titled 'The Right to Write'.

I found it to be a good read. It was wonderful, just learning and getting permission to write and it helped me to understand how to write and inspired me to produce some of my own.

OUR VAIKUṆṬHA PLANET

As I started writing, I decided to read another book by Julia Cameron, called 'The Artist's Way'. Cameron suggested there, it was a good idea to write every day, and so following that cue, over the past 13 years, I've kept up more than 150 notebooks, diaries and journals.

I think these writing books pretty much consolidated my inclination to write this book and to pursue my vocation as an author.

Up until now, despite all this free-writing, I had never actually published anything. So this was a new thing for me completely, to try and publish my first book. And in doing this, as I am, it is a wonderful and enjoyable experience. Now, just moving forward, about a year ago, I enrolled on 13 multi-millionaire programmes.

One of them I followed through, but I didn't get anywhere with it. I then followed another one, then another one, then another one. Then finally, I hit on, one of the programmes I enrolled on, which was Vishal Morjaria's Wow Book Camp, in which I attended a 3-day event spanning the Friday, Saturday and Sunday.

Vishal taught me how to put my book together. Of course, I found that to be an amazing experience and it is that which has led me to write my first book, or speak my first book, actually. That is definitely the best way to start, I found.

I was feeling very anxious about what to call my book and what it would be about. I began thinking I should write all about my life, but then I thought that was a bit misconceived to write all about myself. What I really wanted to write about was how to establish a Vaikuṇṭha planet out of this Earth planet. That may have seemed a little big, at the time, and something my psychiatrist would have something to say about, and most certainly my brother had a lot to say about it. His realistic views, however, regarding my current capabilities, helped me to focus on the most important parts first.

What was important was to write about something closer to home, which was how I coped with anxiety. I had already constructed in my mind, and wrote down a whole series of chapter headings on how to create a Vaikuṇṭha planet, out of this Earth planet. Then a whole series of bullet points for each chapter.

OUR VAIKUṆṬHA PLANET

Altogether, I wrote nine chapter titles and about seven or eight bullet points for each chapter, so, in all, 70 bullet points for the whole book. I thought this was a little bit too much after my brother checked in with me again and went through my book plan. He, his usual way, reminded me that I was not yet ready for such a big task.

I ended up writing about something that I was feeling at the time, which was being anxious about writing a book. And so this is how this book was born. It has turned out to be about the very big and the very small, and everything in between.

So, why do I need to kill even an ant, unnecessarily? If we truly love God, we will not want to kill anyone or anything, for thine is thy glory in heaven and on earth. We will see the Supreme Lord in all creatures and we will be a friend to all of them. That is true love of God.

We will be at peace with ourselves and all God's creation and not want to harm even an ant. I believe that the time is coming when there will be peace on earth, and all men will be at peace with themselves and their fellow human beings.

We simply have to work together to make it happen. If we encroach upon someone else's property, we become cockroaches in our next life. It's that simple. The Lord's kingdom is unlimitedly bountiful, and there's no need to take anybody else's things.

The Good Lord God provides for billions of animals, birds, fishes and all types of living entities. So why would He not provide for me? He will and He does, for sure. So let us give up our greed, our pride, our ego, and our lethargy, and just surrender unto Him and make Him our life and soul and thus we will inherit the kingdom of God on Earth.

What was really happening was just me applying my book to myself, and as I applied myself to my book, I got over my anxiety. The best way I found to get over it was to interact with someone.

It so happened that on one occasion, I was laying in my bed at about four o'clock in the morning, and I was feeling uneasy. Later on, my brother told me that it was possible that

OUR VAIKUṆṬHA PLANET

I felt anxious because I was thinking too big, that I was thinking beyond anything that was within my means, and I needed to scale down. Upon agreeing with him, I found that sudden relief, which led me to write something a bit more reasonable.

I then went back to the drawing board and wrote out a few more titles that were new for my book, and called it all kinds of things. Nevertheless, in the end, I realized the best thing I could just call it was how I cope with anxiety. As you can see that was changed once again.

I finally settled on *Our Vaikuṇṭha Planet*, which felt the most comfortable at the time. It would help anyone who had had anxiety. Because of this, the reference to the words *Vaikuṇṭha planet* in the final title was to be there.

The eight chapters I wrote out were laid out as follows:

❖ *Chapter One –*

    ❏ *People, Politics and Philosophy*

❖ *Chapter Two –*

    ❏ *A Breath of Fresh Air, Action Point*

- ❖ *Chapter Three –*

  - ❑ *A Winter's Hot Drink*

- ❖ *Chapter Four –*

  - ❑ *The Right to Write, Learning To Express Yourself.*

- ❖ *Chapter Five –*

  - ❑ *Rest, Every Endeavour Requires A Rest*

- ❖ *Chapter Six-*

  - ❑ *God, Meditation, and How we can focus our minds on Him*

- ❖ *Chapter Seven –*

  - ❑ *Not doing anything silly.*

My brother suggested calling chapter seven *"Even Keel"*. I wasn't quite sure what he meant by that. He explained that it's like the oyster and seeing the pearl in the oyster. Finally, the last chapter, chapter eight is *"Smile"*. I wanted to put a smile on everyone's face who gets to read this. After my visit to Waterstone's in the middle of writing this book,

I realized that I had picked up 14 books on anxiety.

Altogether, there were maybe about 30 books that they had on my subject that I had written about; there is a lot of information on the subject already.

I felt a little bit overwhelmed by having to read it all. Therefore, what I did was to go through the most up-to-date book on anxiety that was selling the most. It was a book by Sarah Wilson called *First We Make the Beast Beautiful*, which was on living with anxiety.

It had been well received by her blogging and people were buying her book. When I found out about that, and looked at the other books that were on my pile, I realized that what I really wanted to do with my book was to show how to cope with anxiety the spiritual way. I had a real think over my whole plan for the book and realized that what I had originally intended for my book was to create a Vaikuṇṭha planet by establishing a Varnasrāma College, and I had set out eight chapters on that.

After I completed one chapter of five bullet points, I realized that the best thing I could do was to continue in that vein and produce what I was originally intending; in this way "How to Establish a Varnasrāma College" became the last part of my book.

And sitting on top of that would be a chapter, which I originally thought was to be the whole book, "How I Cope with Anxiety" or "How to Cope with Anxiety". Following those chapters would be something else that I had in mind with another chapter after. Therefore, I decided that the best thing I could do is have my book in four parts. Two parts were clear to me; the first part, which will come at the end of the book, would focus on how to establish a Varnasrāma College.

The second part of the book would concern how to cope with anxiety, focusing specifically on the differing aspects of mental health. My mathematics, where I put in the secret life of 50 formulas, would follow. A following small discussion would contain a discursive input on how mathematics can help create peace and unity in the world.

Then, on top of that, the beginning of my book would be on Saṃskṛta, the oldest language in the world, which I had done some work on over the years. I don't know how you feel about that, but this is what I had in mind for the book. For the title of the book, I felt I could call it *My* or *Our Vaikuṇṭha Planet;* Vaikuṇṭha as I was saying before, means, in two parts: *Vai,* meaning *No* and *Kuntha* meaning *Anxiety.* Put together: no anxiety for 8 billion people. But that seemed a little daunting at this stage. I just called my book *Our Vaikuṇṭha Planet.* My subtitle was *From Kṛṣṇa to Varnasrāma.* Kṛṣṇa would contain everything concerning in Samskrta that I was writing right at the front of the book, and then followed by a chapter on mathematics.

Then the third part was on how to cope with anxiety and mental health. And the last part was to be on how to establish a Varnasrāma College. The subtitle would be from Kṛṣṇa *to Varnasrāma.* This is how I planned it. But I don't know how you feel and what you would suggest and advise.

Just to add to the chapter on "How to Cope with Anxiety and Mental Health"; I've put a little bit more at the end of that chapter. It reads as follows:

"The medication they prescribe for mental health problems may or may not be perfect; it is, I would argue, a safety net, and one you cannot afford to do without. You must have adequate safeguards in place to protect your health for sustainable living.

Mental health is, in my view, just about one thing, taking your medication. If you agree to take it, you survive. If you don't, you don't. It's taken me 30 years to realize that and so I'm still here. As Kṛṣṇa says in Bhagavad-gita (9.16),

> "I am the healing herb that calms the mind. So we have to make use of what Kṛṣṇa has provided for our benefit, then we become fighting fit against the forces of evil that might be lurking in our minds."

As I worked on my book, I realised that there was much more to say in some places and much less in others, and so, I have kept much of the main aspects of the book, from the title to the chapters the same with a little variation on content. I am glad to say that as I grew during my journey of overcoming my anxiety, the book as well as the guidance in it grew along with me. I present this book to you now with some pride, satisfaction and joy. My relief from anxiety is as abundant as ever and I believe that this book will help you too.

CHAPTER 1

Discovering That I Was a Paranoid Schizophrenic

My Work Life

If you haven't already gathered, I would like to first of all say that I've been diagnosed as a paranoid schizophrenic for 35 years of my life. With this diagnosis came a list of complicated medications known as mood sedatives such as largatil, chlorpromazine, depixol and many more.

You could say it all started in about 1983 when I joined the Hare Kṛṣṇa temple at Bhaktivedanta Manor, George Harrison's estate in Hertfordshire, U.K. *After that, I became a complete nervous wreck, and that was when the meds began.* I ended up in hospital after having a complete nervous breakdown. For 35 years after that time, I was in and out of hospital regularly, trying to keep a semblance of normality, by trying my hand at a large number of professions, maybe 12 in all. I was constantly seeking to improve myself, but because I couldn't overcome what I thought were the side-effects of the medication for paranoid schizophrenia, I was not able to maintain my positions for very long. Hence me working for 12 different public and private sector organisations in 35 years.

I was constantly feeling tired and lacking in energy and so I had to sleep up to 18 hours a day and a lot of the time my mind was just blank. I could not think or feel very much at all. It was like being in a vegetative state with full body function but no escape from the blankness of my mind.

I was taking on positions which required me to think clearly and use my initiative a lot of the time, but I was in no fit state to continue each time and so I had to keep chopping and changing my career. The hospital authorities were constantly asking me to give up trying to work and relax, which I thought I was, but each time it led to too much pressure and so I ended up at square one.

I was a lost soul in search of my calling and my vocation in life, but with no mind to manage myself. My mind was suffering from mental exhaustion and fatigue.

At last, after all these years, I finally found what I really wanted to do, and that is to write books, or, at least, share my experience and knowledge with other people.

At the time of my searching and growing and my breakdown to my various breakthroughs in life, acting on the suggestions of the hospital authorities, I joined a large number of groups in the hospital, which they thought would help as they tried to assist in getting Humpty Dumpty back together again.

My Experience: I think the one thing that really helped me realize more than anything else, when I was in hospital, was to take the medication. That's the one thing that I found very difficult to do for many, many years. But it became the most important aspect to me in dealing with my mental health, despite not realizing it for many years.

So the 1st point you need to note and work on is:

❖ *Take your Medication every day as prescribed.*

If I had just agreed to taking the medication and realising that it would be half *'placebo effect'*, and half *'active principle'* then I would maybe have been able to avoid 30 years of being in and out of hospital and may have been able to sustain a stable job for 30 years. Hindsight is always a good thing. However, it was maybe due to my misunderstanding of how the mind works, that led to all the troubles.

From the Bhagavad-gita, I had learnt that the mind is more subtle than the gross body, so how could something that is gross, namely, chemicals, possibly help my subtle mind. With this thought blocking my openness to the possibility that the medication would be successful, I was convinced at the time that medication was of no use to me.

I struggled with that for a long time. Until I realised, from reading my spiritual master's book called, Srimad Bhagavatam, that whatever problem one may have in this world, if we simply go to the authority on that problem, you will find the solution for sure. For my upset mind and me, the authority was my psychiatrist. What the psychiatrist was telling me was what I should have been doing sometime before.

Because I was rebelling against the whole idea of taking medication and thinking, *"Why do I need it? There's nothing wrong with my mind, I don't need medication, I don't need the side effects of sleeping up to 18 hours a day, and the doctors are telling me I must take painful and annoying injections all the time."*

Little did I realise that it was not the medication that made me sleep for up to 18 hours a day; rather it was the mental fatigue that my mind was experiencing from all the strain of studying up to 18 hours. I did this every day from the age of 6 up until the age of 24, which led to my complete nervous breakdown.

I would blame the medication and repeat to myself that the medication was the problem repeatedly for quite some considerable time, over 30 years in fact. Yet each time I would end up with a relapse and have to go back into the hospital. Eventually, I realized that if I just do what my psychiatrist was telling me, which was to take the medication, everything would be okay. And it was.

Discovering That I Had Anxiety

"Talking about my own anxiety made me feel a lot lighter in myself."

I had never felt anxious for the first 45 years of my life. I never knew what anxiety really was and I never really understood what people meant when they said they were anxious, because I had never felt it myself. Then, when I felt anxious for the very first time, it was like a bolt out the blue.

It was when I was left on my own for a long period, without my brother. He had gone to India, and I was left to fend for myself, in my one bedroom flat in Willesden. Suddenly because I had no one to talk to, I felt very, very anxious. At first I didn't know what to do, but then I thought about calling the Samaritans. It was then that I realized, when I did speak to someone on the other end of the phone, in about 10-15 minutes of speaking, I became completely pacified.

I completely became non-anxious again, and it was a wonderful experience, because prior to that, I was feeling extreme un-ease.

I had no idea why it had occurred and how I came to feel that way, but it was extremely unpleasant; as one person put it, *"It was the disease that came with the un-ease that was consuming me."* This really painful experience was the most unpleasant feeling I had ever had and it felt horrible.

I didn't know how to cope. However, I did find the best way to deal with it and that was simply to speak to someone about it. That was a really defining moment for me at the time and that all came about at the age of 45.

I'm now 60 years old. However, it was in moments of revelations like these that I really found my own up until the present time.

OUR VAIKUṆṬHA PLANET

It was a great turning point for me to realize that whenever I felt anxious, the best thing I could possibly do was to confide in anyone and everyone. Therefore, if there was just one other person I could speak to when I felt anxious, then I knew that would get rid of my anxiety straight away, or within about 10-15 minutes.

My Experience: *When I was Anxious as I was when I started writing this book about how to overcome anxiety, and how to cope with anxiety, the best way which was most helpful was just to speak to someone about it. The 2nd point you need to note and work on is:*

❖ *When you speak to someone about your Anxiety then you'll definitely get over some of it, if not all of it.*

In my case, I got rid of all of it. So it's making the connection, connecting with people, that does the trick. Life is that easy. It's reaching out when you really need to. *'God helps those who help themselves'.*

Having the courage to connect with people when you're feeling anxious will help you take the first steps in overcoming your anxiety. If you can just connect, and realize that the best thing you can ever do when you're feeling anxious, is to connect with someone.

When that connection is there, and a focused live person is communicating with you, both hearing what you have to say and responding to what you have to say, with uninterrupted interaction. Then the anxiety disappears almost automatically and straight away.

That was my one thing that I found very, very helpful. There's a whole range of other things I found useful after that, but I didn't realize what being anxious really meant until then. However, it was at that moment, the moment when I was entirely alone and resorted to calling the Samaritans, that really helped me through my life afterwards.

I had other things that were very helpful. However, this was the main thing that really got me together and got my head together. Thus, that's why I would say connection and connecting with people, REAL PEOPLE, will help 8 Billion People overcome their anxiety.

CHAPTER 2

More About My History and Family

Joining His Divine Grace
A.C. Bhaktivedanta Swami Prabhupada

My parents became attached to *His Divine Grace A.C. Bhaktivedanta Swami Prabhupada*, the founder-acarya of the International Society for Kṛṣṇa Consciousness, or the Hare Kṛṣṇa movement, when I was 9 years old, and a year later, in December 1969, my parents and my two brothers and myself; we became disciples of Srila Prabhupada. We changed a lot of our life from then on after that.

I became totally introverted because of meeting my spiritual master for the first time. For many years, I cut myself completely off from the whole world, and found what I enjoyed more than anything was just studying. At school, I spent all my time studying. And so, I did my 10-O-levels, my 5-A-levels, and my degree at Oxford. Shortly after I worked for GEC Marconi Avionics, for 14 months, and then I joined a master's degree course at Brunel University now in digital systems, which I didn't complete, because at that point in my life I started asking the more fundamental questions in life:

❖ *Who am I?*

❖ *Where have I come from?*

❖ *Where am I going with all this?*

I broke off from studying and joined the Hare Kṛṣṇa temple in Letchmore Heath, and decided to live as a monk for the rest of my life. But it was whilst I was living there that I ended up with a nervous breakdown. I was in and out of hospital for many years after that.

It was quite a traumatic experience, as you can imagine, spending a long chunk of my life in mental health services, and having a completely distraught life, from what I had imagined it to be, after coming out from Oxford. And it was really when I was at Oxford that I started becoming completely confused.

I had done well at my A-Levels. However, after that I went downhill, and I just couldn't think straight, my mind just wasn't able to think properly.

Therefore, even though I enjoyed the engineering science degree that I did, I felt I didn't learn much from it, because my mind was so disturbed. I had wanted to come out with a first class degree that I fully understood.

Therefore, it was because I channelled all my energy into studying, and not learn any social skills that I had so many problems. All my school reports talked about this one thing. My teachers all talked about me not being sociable.

Thus, I ended up being too narrowly focused and completely confused. For a long time, I felt the trauma of being in hospital.

Nevertheless, the good news was that I was able to recover. This whole story is about how I recovered and how I felt after that by learning to cope with panic, which is the extreme end of anxiety: again, by connecting with people. And that's the great revelation that I had more than anything else: *"Connecting with people helps anxiety fade"*.

It was in the groups that I had in the hospital where I found myself again and gained lots of energy and vitality and enthusiasm for life again.

But still I didn't think that I had managed to get over the worst of it until I started taking the medication and realized that if I just took the medication, then things would really improve for me, and they did.

So remember:

❖ **1 Take your medication.**

❖ **2 Talk about your anxiety with others.**

So those are the first things I would suggest for anyone in mental health who has, what the psychiatrists would say, a mental health problem, or issue. If they suggest taking medication, then just take it. "If you can learn to tolerate the so-called side-effects of the meds. The world is your oyster."

It may be worth adding at this point what one of my psychiatrists once told me, and that is there is in the US Supreme Court today, a lady who had paranoid schizophrenia, that lady now sits in as a judge. She is acting as a judge in the Supreme Court of United States of America. *Anything is possible*. Of course, we know about John Nash, who won a Nobel Prize, who for many years, suffered from paranoid schizophrenia.

So we can see that people, even if they have had a mental health problem, they can still get on with their lives successfully and independently.

As John Nash, and his wife as well as the 'A Beautiful Mind' book and film that came out relate, they had a child that also had something similar, but he realized that his child was making his own journey. Which made him realise that he too could become as brilliant as his father was.

So there's no loss. That's all I can say. *"Everyone in mental health knows, there is a fine line which divides genius from madness."* Stepping over that fine line and in which direction determines whether we are accepted or not.

My Brother, My Hero – My Mother, My Smile Master

The next point I would like to make is about having a cheerful disposition to overcoming anxiety. What I'd like to say about that is they say that it takes a lot of energy to have a depressed face, than it does to have a smile on one's face. By just having a smile on your face, you automatically uplift your whole mood and outlook.

Even if you don't feel like it, smiling will help you feel happy. This is how easy it is to be happy. On a more serious note, my mother, Srimati Kirti Ma Devi Dasi had been told she had three to six months to live back in 1979, after she developed breast cancer. At the time, my brother, at the ripe age of 21, stepped up and took responsibility.

He told my mother that he would not study, he would not work, and he would not do anything for himself now as she was his first priority, and he would take care of her full time and so he did. He put a lot of love, support and effort into taking care of my mom and the family as well.

He brought juices, did lots of shopping for her daily needs and provided some medicines. He even got some cow urine, from Bhaktivedanta Manor, which might sound strange, but my mother drank it. She also drank a little caranamrta, which is some bathing stuff, which they make to remove disease at the Manor, and she took some yogurt and some Tulasi leaves (holy basil). That was it. She took the treatment of the doctors as well of course.

I would say she went to Hammersmith Hospital, for all her appointments, and had chemotherapy. Can you believe from being told that you have three to six months to live, she lived another 17 years? The most remarkable thing is that she didn't pass away from cancer at all. It was a mild form of pneumonia, she just got a cold.

And can you believe it?

She kept happy.

She would smile at every chance she had.

OUR VAIKUNTHA PLANET

My mother actually told my father that she would leave her body so that he could get on with his life as a renounced monk, which my father wanted to be; he wanted to take sannyasa, and he wanted to be a sannyasi by order of his spiritual master. My mother said *'when the time comes, I won't get in your way.'*

So a little later, she decided to leave whilst she was working in the garden. If I remember rightly, my father phoned me from India a few months before and told me that my mother hasn't eaten for a month. I immediately said I'm coming over to see her straight away. I took the first plane from London to Delhi and arrived in Delhi. I immediately took a train to Agra where she was in the nursing home.

When I got to Agra, I frantically tried to get the address of which place it was, the rickshaw-wala had no idea where she was or where to go. But I just remembered it was in an Agra nursing home. Therefore, he took me to various other places first. Finally, I arrived at the nursing home, and my mother was there. As soon as I arrived, she embraced me.

I wasted no time as I realised the situation was dire and so I gave her a little medicine that I had bought from London as soon as I could. It was a cintamani medicine of Ayurveda preparation, which I gave her with a little honey. Once she had taken it, I then gave her a little papaya too. She took a few pieces of the papaya.

I then asked, is there anything else I could do? She said, *'Bas'* meaning *'that's enough.'* Whilst everyone around was loudly chanting the Holy Name of the Lord, she passed away, but the point is she kept very happy throughout her life, even after being told that she had not very long to live. That was a wonderful, wonderful revelation and realization for everyone. If you keep happy in this world, you can definitely prolong your life and live on to at least another 17 years. Incidentally, my mother, not long before she passed, asked me to do three things.

She asked me to preach, to which I said, "Yes, I will, Mother." She asked me to write books, to which I said, "I will, Mother, yes." The third thing she asked me to do was to "make disciples"; I said that I would do this also. Thus, my mother left me with these three wonderful instructions. However, it was quite startling when she told me as it was back in 1995. I was only 36 years old and dealing with coping with my work with Brent Council and my mental health. I had agreed, but I spent the next 25 years contemplating how I would fulfil that order. It is now 2019, some 24 years later, and I'm only just starting to realize what my mother told me. Her instructions are now as clear, and as true as ever. My work is becoming easier, with a mind that can finally think, making her dream for me a reality. I have her blessings and her support to actually fulfil my life as if she asked me to do.

My Experience: My Blessed Mother has showed me that if you keep smiling you will be happy.

So the Third point you need to note and work on is:

❖ *Smile until you are happy. Keeping a cheerful disposition is definitely the way forward for everyone. The more you smile the happier you will be and the longer you will live.*

So just do that right now. You will see the difference between being miserable and being happy straightaway. So we have to have fun with whatever we do in life. It is having the enthusiasm, the determination, the patience, and the confidence. If we have enough enthusiasm to do we want to do in life we will definitely achieve it. Therefore, it's having that sense of play and fun and happiness that will lead to the bliss that we're really looking for. Then life becomes a lot easier and all the struggles and difficulties that we put ourselves through become a joy.

Try this joke.

Why is it dangerous to play in the jungle?

I don't know?

Because there are too many cheetahs!

How Philosophy Can Help

The next thing I had on my list for trying to rid yourself, or free yourself from anxiety, or just becoming less anxious, was to develop a philosophy or idea of not harming anyone or anything. And that's it, actually it was Lord

Buddha's idea. Ahimsa Paro Dharmo, the greatest religion, is not to hurt or harm anyone or anything.

It's a case of what comes around goes around, or what goes around comes around. By having a simple life, and living simply and thinking highly, we can actually become very peaceful, in ourselves, very, very peaceful and happy.

By living on a very simple plant based diet, if we just eat things that naturally grow out of the ground, like fruits and vegetables, and just survive on milk and water, and all the wonderful juices, that is sufficient to keep the body nourished, and that will prolong the life. It's going back to being in tune with nature.

You Are What You Eat, They Say.

By just having simple things, natural things, which don't harm any living entity, in particular, animals, or birds or fishes, then man can live in tune with nature and prolong his life. We don't, as far as I can see, need to eat animals, birds, or fishes of any sort. Even if we had no other choice, if we allow them to die naturally, and then eat them, then that would be the best policy.

34

Man Mohan Gupta

Because all living entities have a right to live, and even plants, animals, birds and trees, they all have a right to live. The consciousness is always evolving.

It is what the Bible says and what the Quran says, and what the Dharmapada says, and what the Bhagavad-gita says, if you offer a fruit, a flower, a leaf, or some water, to Kṛṣṇa, or to the Supreme Personality of Godhead, and you offer it with love and devotion, He will definitely accept it.

So by actually offering things that are very simple, and that don't require killing any living entities unnecessarily, then the Lord's very pleased with that.

And it helps us to keep a clear, clean life in our own minds. We are then able to think about doing good for all other people, and indeed, all other living entities. So Lord Buddha has preached «Ahimsa» or nonviolence. But that means not just to other human beings, but to all living entities.

We have to see how we can live in a simple way, by just the basic ingredients, which will help us to nourish our body completely. So a large part of the world's population will survive just by things coming out of the ground, and milk and water and so on. If we can keep the balance of the ecology of the planet together, by maintaining a stable order that will certainly please the Supreme Lord. The Supreme Lord is controlling the whole nature of all the animals, of all the birds, of all the fishes, so it doesn't matter what man does to try to interfere with that.

❖ *Man has managed to accelerate death and destruction, but can he accelerate life or, may I say, create it, even?*

❖ *If we cannot produce life, what right do we have to end it?*

The Supreme Lord will automatically control the populations of all these living entities and He does. As far as we are concerned, we have only to worry about our life and how to live it, not the unnecessary killing of any other living entities. That's all. And so, if we keep in check, how we ourselves are living, and then automatically everything else becomes properly organized by the control of the Supreme Lord.

If we just think for a moment whose nature this is that we talked about, we will very quickly conclude it can only be God's nature, His mighty power and splendour and dominion over all that be.

If we don't cheat with God's nature, and if we eat what is set aside for us by Him, and not harm any other living entities, then we won't have any bad karma, or bad reaction. If we don't have that, then there less likely chance of being anxious about what's happening to us in the world today.

As many people, like Mahatma Gandhi, said, that if we want to get rid of all the wars, and the famines and all the pestilence in the world, then we have to get rid of the dog eat dog mentality that we've developed.

If we just simply eat things that don't require killing a dog, or a cat, or an animal, a cow, or a pig, or sheep, or fish, or bird, these things are moving, talking and living entities, they have a higher consciousness, to plants and trees, and things that grow from the ground. So, if things that have a higher level of consciousness are killed and eaten, then we have to suffer for that. The Lord has set aside, what is acceptable to Him, something we can all manage on. And if we abide by that, then we become free from our karma.

We become free from our karma, by offering back those things which the Lord has set aside for us.

So if we can just live simply on the planet, then the whole planet will become like a paradise. It will become a Vaikuṇṭha planet. 'Vai' means 'no' and «kuntha» means 'anxiety', no anxiety for 8 billion people. So that's possible, if we live simply. And it's very, very healthy. I'm now 60. And I admit I'm very fat. Because of all the eating I've done, so it's something that I have to keep in check. But I've been vegetarian practically all my life.

Before I became a Hare Kṛṣṇa devotee, I must admit, I did eat meat then. But after that, I gave up eating meat, and fish and eggs. And I haven't looked back since. Although, when I was in hospital, I must admit, I did. I did resort to eating a piece of a fish once. It was something I regret now.

Man Mohan Gupta

However, I was very ill at that time, mentally. And most people are, well, not in a hospital. So, you don't need to eat meat, fish and eggs. It's possible to live a happy, peaceful life, just by being vegetarian, and offering your food stuffs to the Lord. Like when I was at school, we all offered grace to the Lord. I don't know if they still do that in schools. When I was in the infants, before we ate our meals, we said grace. I think that's a very good thing offering our foodstuffs to the Lord before we eat them, it makes us feel grateful for what we have received.

We become happy and nourished at the same time, it's like medicine, if you know it's going to work, half of it is thinking that it will work, it's the placebo effect given by the doctor. So, if we eat something that we're grateful for, and we haven't killed, then we nourish our bodies nicely, and we develop nice brain tissues. And it's a wonderful thing. So, this is what I would like to say about that, thank you! The Hare Kṛṣṇa's, as we all know, are famous for chanting and dancing and giving out foodstuffs.

They are known as the kitchen religion sometimes because they keep giving out food-stuffs to anyone and everyone, and it is with a view to getting peace in this world, and developing love of God, so that everyone becomes happy.

We may not necessarily want to chant Hare Krsna, or chant Krsna's name, because we may not know what that means, but if we chant Allah or Jehovah or Yahweh, or Jesus, we will get the same benefit, because ultimately, it's the same God that we're all worshiping. By keeping a firm faith in the Lord, whoever we think He is, then we'll get benefit from that. Nevertheless, Krsna appeared 5246 years ago on the planet, and He performed some wonderful pastimes, which you can read about in the Krsna book, which my spiritual master, translated from Samskrta into English about 50 years ago.

The most important thing that comes to mind at this point, is developing good habits and learning new habits that will help a person develop in this life. By developing good habits, always thinking when you wake up in the morning *'What good habit will I learn today'?*

It's always being in a mood, of wanting to learn something new every day, seeing what's new and challenging yourself: *'What am I going to learn today?'* As one writer wrote, what is a life if you haven't examined yourself, and you haven't strived to find out and tried to reach a higher position than you are already in?

So what is the point of heaven if you haven't tried to reach there? I forget how he said it now, but, in essence, he said that it's always seeking to strive for a higher and higher place. It's a very nice and interesting phrase.

> *"Ah, but a man's reach should exceed his grasp, or what's a heaven for."*
>
> — *Browning.*

So it's a matter of developing good habits in life, which will help everyone and Steve Jobs famously said, that it's only people who are really mad, who actually change the world. In the end, they're mad enough to think they can change the world, that they as you do change the world in the end.

So it's seeing how we can do that, by learning good habits, one step at a time, little by little. *This is the idea:* All great people, all the great inspiring leaders, all the great educators, all the great technologists, they've all strived to improve people's lives. And they've done that by developing good habits. They've, I'm sure, felt anxious, a lot along the way, in what they've tried to achieve. But they have come out successful, because they've been able to concentrate their minds on a focused target. And so, if we concentrate our efforts and minds on *F.O.C.U.S.: Follow One Course Until Successful, then we'll definitely be successful*. It is because we stray from focusing on one object, one course that we actually end up doing so many other things. Kṛṣṇa in Bhagavad-gita, explains,

man-mana bhava mad-bhakto
mad-yaji mam namaskuru

Always think of Me, become My devotee, offer your obeisances unto Me, offer your homage unto Me and definitely you will come back to Me.

Therefore, by concentrating our mind on Kṛṣṇa, everything becomes normalized. By following God's path, one actually becomes very successful in life. We see that with so many people who followed that path, the great leaders, successful business people, and even actors, because they concentrated their mind on the Supreme Lord they achieved the highest perfection of life.

So remember:

❖ 1 Take your medication.

❖ 2 Talk about your anxiety with others.

❖ 3 Smile until you are happy.

❖ 4 The philosophy or idea of not harming anyone or anything.

CHAPTER 3

More Recent Discoveries to My Anxiety

A Breath of Fresh Air

Another thing I did to get over my anxiety was, my brother said, open the windows to my flat. And that was just the other day, I was feeling very anxious. I didn't feel like moving. But my brother opened one window, and I felt very lethargic and very reluctant. But I did manage to get up and open the other one.

As a result, I felt very good about that. It was like I opened the window to my life, this was about five o'clock in the morning, and it was still quite dark then. It felt wonderful. It allowed me to breathe a lot freer. I realized that just by doing what my brother told me to do, that helped enormously, getting a breath of fresh air into the flat and getting fresh air into my lungs. So it was appreciating nature. And appreciating nature is very important at the best of times, or even at the worst of times, as it was for me then.

I was feeling very low, because of my anxiety. Appreciating nature by having some fresh air coming onto me, that was wonderful. Just being able to appreciate the sun's ray and the light it brought upon me, the warmth of the sunshine or the cooling rays of the moon when it's out.

There was a time just recently when I was staring at the moon at night. It was a bit like pictures you see in children's books sometimes, where there's a face, on the moon, in the shape of a crescent, with a little nose sticking out from the crescent, I could see the eyes on the crescent of the moon in the sky, a little nose sticking out.

It was a wonderful feeling. It was a golden banana actually, that I felt like eating.

When I sometimes see the sun it reminds me of when *Kṛṣṇa says, in Bhagavad-gita, "He is the light of the sun and the moon" ("prabhasmi sasi-suryayoh»)* (Bg. 7.8) It's appreciating Kṛṣṇa's energies in this world. The light of the sun and the moon is definitely Kṛṣṇa's energy, which *really helps.*

My Experience: So getting a breath of fresh air, appreciating nature, and appreciating the creation of the Lord, through the sun, the moon, the stars, and the planets, definitely helps the mind and gets rid of some of my anxieties.

So the 5th point you need to note and work on is:

❖ *Take deep breaths of fresh air when you open a window and really feel the sun or moon rays being absorbed by your skin.*

It gets rid of the un-ease, I'd mentioned before, the unease which is a little bit of the dis-ease that creates tension in the mind. That's ultimately what leads to physical problems. They are psychosomatic, the mind has problems, and so it comes out in the body.

So if we can heal our minds, then our physical body becomes relaxed and relieved. This is it, if we feel in the mind it is something that we can overcome, and again, through all these methods, I'm suggesting, to overcome the disease, then that will get over the physical disease that we have in the body, because the body at the end of the day has come about because of the mind.

The subtle body of the mind, intelligence and false ego leads to the physical body, of the hands, the legs, and the arms and so on. The gross body comes about because of the subtle body, and the subtle body is a covering of the soul.

Faith and Spirituality – the friend when you are alone

The soul is something that also has a form, a spiritual form, a spiritual body. An example that can be given is that of a glove: it has shape because the hand has shape. So, if the hand did not have shape, then the glove would have no shape. So similarly, the soul has a spiritual form. That's why we have a physical form our self.

We have a subtle form in the mind. Then when that is developed it comes out into a physical body. So, understanding what our spiritual form is, that is what life is about, knowing who we are, as spiritual beings, with a spiritual form, our true identity and our activities, what we are supposed to be doing, as spiritual beings on this planet. And by understanding our spiritual identity, we can actually engage in spiritual activities and then interact on a spiritual level. So that's very important. And that's how we can get unity and harmony and peace and wonderful relationships across the planet. It is getting rid of the un-ease and dis-ease of the mind.

So this is what we're talking about when we try and practice Kṛṣṇa consciousness, or what the high Kṛṣṇa devotees are practicing, they are trying to get rid of the dis-ease of the mind and become at ease with themselves, understanding their transcendental form, in relationship to the Supreme form, which is the Supreme Lord.

OUR VAIKUṆṬHA PLANET

The Lord has His transcendental form. And we as His parts and parcels also have our transcendental form. How we can invoke that transcendental form of ours is by engaging in His unalloyed service. And that's the process of devotion, bhakti yoga. Yoga means to link with the Supreme Lord. And we do that in service, by service activity.

Many years ago, I came across a very wonderful book called *Friends Are Forever*. I just recently found out who it's written by. Jessica Taylor writes it in very small print. It's a miniature book, the size of too match boxes, or even smaller. It's a wonderful book, and I've had it with me for many years.

I found that very helpful and comforting.

Whenever I felt like having a friend, and knowing what it is to be a friend, I would take out this book and remind myself of what it said. So it's got some wonderful things in it. Maybe about 70 different sayings about friendship. And it's something I found very helpful and comforting in the last 20 years. And so I thought I'd recommend that book.

Man Mohan Gupta

It's printed in 2001 by Irresistible books, and published by Small World Books, a division of Small World Publishing. I learned so much about how to be a friend to myself, primarily; then, if I want a friend, I have to be a friend. For many years, for practically all my life, I felt I had never had a friend. The only person that really spoke to me was my brother. He's been with me for the last 60 years. After Kṛṣṇa, apart from being my brother, he is clearly my best friend. He has been everything to me. Reading this book, *Friends Are Forever*, it highlighted for me what a friend really is. One thing it says is:

"Be civil to all, sociable to many, familiar with a few, friend to one, enemy to none."

— Benjamin Franklin.

"Am I not killing my enemies when I make friends with them?"

— Abraham Lincoln.

I like to quote that one a lot. There's so many nice sayings in that book. I found them all very useful. When I have nothing to think about I just refer to my little book and it puts a smile on my face. This is another way to get rid of anxiety or being anxious.

So the 6th point you need to note and work on is:

The 7 Mini steps to get rid of your anxiety. By answering the following questions, you will write your own seven steps to get rid of your anxiety.

> *6.1. Who have you spoken to about it?*
>
> *6.2. What have they said?*
>
> *6.3. How do you want to follow that up?*
>
> *6.4. When do you plan on doing that?*
>
> *6.5. Where will you be when you are free from your anxiety?*
>
> *6.6. Why can't you get rid of it now?*
>
> *6.7. Who, What, How, When, Where and Why can't you celebrate now?*

My Experience:

6.1. My brother,

6.2. *Don't worry. Open the window. Get some fresh air. Have a hot drink. Write down how you feel. Relax and take rest. Meditate on Kr.s.n.a. Keep on an even keel. Smile!*

6.3. *Action stations*

6.4. *Right now.*

6.5. *In the same place but free in my head.*

6.6. *I have.*

6.7. *I am telling my brother straight-away that I am free from my anxiety.*

So those are some of the questions and some answers that you can think about.

CHAPTER 4

How the World Affects Anxiety

Seasons and the Effect
They Have on Anxiety.

Now what we really need in winter is something to warm the cockles of the heart. And what I found very helpful, when I was feeling cold and miserable and full of anxiety was to have something hot, which my brother made up again, which was a wonderful ginger drink.

He heated up some water, put some ginger in it. And then he put something else in it, some herbs or something. A nice little brand of cane sugar, and then when I drank it, I felt so relieved. It was wonderful. That immediately helped my anxiety that I was feeling. So just having a hot warm drink, and having natural herbs. Natural spices, if you like, in your drink, will clean out your colonics and give you the flow that you're looking for, it's like a river going down to the sea. As soon as it's unblocked, it flows very smoothly, and it comes down to the sea. But if it collects, the whole land gets cluttered, and it gets all over the place.

So it's unblocking and digging out the weeds in our heart. And that's what life is about really, is digging out the weeds that we've accumulated, or cobwebs that we've accumulated over so many days, weeks, months and years, it's clearing out the weeds of our heart. *If we are open to that, there's a process by which we can do it.*

That's the science of self-realization, realizing ourselves to our fullest potential. That's the process we're suggesting, as a means to helping our anxiety. There is a book called *The Science of Self-realization by His Divine Grace, A.C. Bhaktivedanta Swami Prabhupada; it's a tremendous read.* I read it many years ago, and I found it very, very helpful. It's something which really helped me to understand a little bit more about myself, about things in the world in general, the structure of society, and it had things on astrology and astronomy, as well. For example, it mentioned that if you have a tree, you have to judge it by the result it gives, that is, by the fruit it gives. These things are all there.

Not every tree is going to give you a sweet mango. So, every fruit that comes out from a tree can be utilized in some way or another. It's seeing the all pervasiveness of the wonderful creation of the Lord, in its full magnanimity.

And by seeing that, and appreciating that, we become less anxious, we become more grateful, we become more pleased within ourselves. We are then able to carry on with our life in a wonderful way. So this is how we can carry on. In addition, it's like, for example, if we drink water, which is so harmless and pure, it's a wonderful way of cleansing the body. These things are very simple, but we tend to forget what to do when we're anxious.

So, by sometimes having a little reminder, either by someone else telling us, or reading a book or just recalling something someone may have once told us that can make all the difference in the end. If we simply muster up the courage to listen to what is being said, then, very quickly, we can become free. Therefore, it's doing things like that that will help us more than anything else.

A recap of the points to work on so far:

Mark off with yes or no, what has helped you since you started.

1. **Take your medication.**

2. **Talk about your anxiety with others.**

3. **Smile until you are happy.**

4. **The philosophy or idea of not harming anyone or anything.**

5. **Take deep breaths of fresh air when you open a window, really feel the sun or moon rays being absorbed by your skin.**

6. **The 7 Mini steps to get rid of your anxiety, by answering the following questions; you will write your own seven steps to getting rid of it.**

a. Who have you spoken to about your anxiety?

_____

b. What have they said?

_____

_____

_____

c. How do you want to follow that up?

_____

d. When do you plan on doing that?

_____

e. Where will you be when you are free from your anxiety?

_____

f. Why can't you get rid of it now?

_____

g. Who, What, How, When, Where and Why can't you celebrate now?

_____

7. *Take a winter's hot drink to warm the heart*

CHAPTER 5

Taking Action

The Writer in You

One thing that I found very helpful when I was anxious was just to do something; get busy, to get myself out of what I was thinking.

My Experience: What I found useful was to write, just give myself permission to write about how I felt.

So the Eighth point you need to note and work on is:

8. *Write, Read, Listen*

   a. **Write** *a journal of your feelings to keep track of* **how you feel**

about the things going on in your
life and identify what effects
they are having on your anxiety
levels

b. Read books that will distract you,
teach you, and calm you when you
are experiencing anxiety.

c. Listen to some calming music or
the sounds of Nature to r*elax your
mind.*

Writing my feelings was relieving and
especially liberating. It gave me the power of
self-expression, which is creative, and it got me
out of my downward spiral. It may take a little practice, but if you can mutter up enough
energy to write, then you'll find that the pain
that you're feeling will ease.

*Or, if you can't write, you can just read. And
if you don't want to read, you can just listen.
Listen to some wonderful calming music.*

Sometimes, I listened to 432 hertz deep calming music, which you can listen to as you fall
asleep. These things are there. It's a wonderful
way of relaxing, and just seeing how you can

use whatever is available to bring about that all-illusive calm that is definitely there within us.

Reflection

What I found most of all helpful was being able to speak to someone. Quite often, they would suggest then putting on some music. Or something else like, one thing I found very helpful was to reflect on what I'd done in the past.

My Experience: I reflected on when I was a lot younger, how I started to learn to read and write and do arithmetic, just basic things about how I came to be the way I am now through introspection, meditation and education.

Those things were very helpful to just reflect on the past, and be able to see them in a positive light, to gradually see that all these things that had happened to me, they had all been for a reason. It is introspection and reflection like this, which a form of self-education that forms part of the process of self-realization.

So the ninth point you need to note and work on is:

❖ *Take the time to reflect on what's hap-pened in your life, and see how you can make something of it today.*

Not everything that's happened to us in the past will have been good. We will have defi-nitely experienced some things that have upset us, which may have disturbed us for some time. But it's seeing how those same things actually are the means by which we solve our problems today. It's like a vaccination or inoculation, injecting a little germ in the body. Then that becomes the fighting mechanism by which you counteract that same disease in the body. It's a well-known thing, in homeopathy, for example, they introduce a little bit of the same germ to fight the majority, thus boosting the immune system. Another example is eating too many sweets.

If you have eaten too many milk sweets, then you can eat another milk product, yogurt, which has bacteria in it, which will counteract the problem that was there in the first place. So it's utilizing whatever's causing the problem in a slightly different way to counteract the original problem.

It is just tweaking the system, tweaking the mind, so that you get the result that you're looking for. That can make all the difference. Generally, help is always at hand – it's asking for it when we most need it. Ask and you shall receive. It's seeing how we can do that in our own life, to good effect.

I've found that very helpful many times in the past. Just seeing how a little bit of change is enough to work out the negativity, breaking the vicious cycle I have got myself into, and now looking at it in a positive way, which may just be the last straw to get me back on an even keel and so improve my life. It's having faith that things will get better and so they do.

My mother once said to me, 'It doesn't matter how difficult it gets, and never give up. Never give up.' So it's like that. We have to keep persevering in life. There's a great deal to live for. We will come out from the darkness, if we persevere; it's just doing that when the chips are down.

OUR VAIKUṆṬHA PLANET

Creativity, Faith and Inspiration

If we are struggling with creativity and seeing how we can continue to produce something as good as what we have just done, then the thing to do is to remember the Supreme Lord.

My Experience: In Bhagavad-gita (15.15), Kṛṣṇa says, "sarvasya caham hrdi sannivistho mattah smrtir jnanam apohanam ca". What that means is that the Lord is the source of all our knowledge, our remembrance, and our forgetfulness.

So when we remember the Lord again, then all the creative juices that we had flowing, they all start to flow again.

So the tenth point you need to note and work on is:

❖ *Remember the Lord and He will inspire you, He will help your creative juices flow again. Even if you do not fully believe in Him His magic will enhance your inspiration.*

He then becomes the source of our knowledge, and everything that we're trying to achieve in our life. So, by doing that, by remembering the Lord, all our creative flow comes back on tap again. He gives us the power to be able to continue. All inspiration and intuition is coming from the Supersoul, the Lord sitting in our heart.

All the great composers, artists, writers, scientists and people in general, we all get our inspiration from within, ultimately; so when we have a brain-wave, that's all coming from the Supreme Lord. Even if we don't believe in the Lord, we have to rely on inspiration, coming from within and without, to continue with our life. So if we do that, by thinking of the Lord at a time when we feel blocked, at a time when we think we can't carry on, that's when the Lord really helps.

When We Reach Out, Then Kr.s.n.a Comes to the Rescue

He comes to the rescue like International Rescue in Thunderbirds that I used to see when I was about six. It was a great programme, because there would be a great deal of conflict and they would have a real problem on their hands, initially. All very touch and go, but then the five Thunderbirds would come to the rescue, and they would always come out victorious.

There are a lot of the programmes I used to see apart from Thunderbirds, Batman, and Mission Impossible. I'm just trying to think - there were other programmes, like the Saint. They all had an element of conflict, but there was a hero or heroine that would ultimately solve the problem. I use to find those programmes very exciting.

When there's a great deal of conflict and you wonder what's going to happen. But that's what makes a good story. It's seeing how we can translate what we have seen on the screen to solving the real- life conflicts that we have in our real life, by remembering the Lord in such time to genuinely come and help us. That is real International Rescue or Universal Rescue. It does work, and it's something I can confess that has definitely helped me time and time again in my life.

CHAPTER 6

Nurturing the Body, Nurtures the Mind

Every Endeavour Requires a Rest

One thing I found very interesting is that when I haven't had enough sleep, my mind becomes a little disturbed. I become confused and I can't think straight, I can't act and I can't do anything, simply because of a lack of sleep. At that point, the first thing I do is find a spot where I can just lie down and relax. And take a quick power nap, it's exactly what I've just done actually.

My Experience: I was working away and speaking to my brother again. But later on about nine o'clock, I started feeling quite queasy, my mind was not working or functioning properly.

So I immediately did my HHH – Horizontal Half Hour, and I took some rest, except I rested from 9 till 12pm, three hours. That was what I really needed to rejuvenate me and my mind after getting up at 4.15 this morning.

So the eleventh point you need to note and work on is:

❖ **Know your body, Keep track of your sleeping patterns and see what works for you. If you get too much sleep it will affect you just a badly as if you get too little sleep. Not everyone needs the same amount of sleep and you need to work out how many hours of sleep has you the most relaxed and refreshed.**

It is knowing what works for you and then taking a quick shower, and that completely rejuvenates everything. So having the right amount of sleep, and having a quick shower, and then eating - these things definitely help the mind and the body to relax, and to think clearly again. And when we're in that state, we're in the zone, again, we are in the flow and back on track. It's pausing for thought, and it's realizing that every endeavour needs a rest.

No one can continue on and on without a rest. That's what I found very helpful. Realizing when my mind is not thinking clearly is to just relax and pause and try and do something different. Or just take a nap. Eat like a bird and sleep like a dog. Nature's ways. Something else that has helped me is Theta healing. This is something that I came across just a few months ago, by one of my mentors.

She introduced it to me (her name is Tatjana Valujeva). She showed me how Theta Healing can heal my body and mind. I rely on the supreme creator to bring about the healing.

There is a method involved. But, ultimately, it is depending on the Supreme Lord, for the result. So, I found that helpful, again, because it involved, in my case, writing things down. And easing the pain that I had in my foot. Although the pain is still there, is definitely getting better.

It's persevering, is realizing by persevering, you will get to your ultimate destination.

Resting and then going back into activity, resting and then going back is like interval training for the mind. It's like all athletes, they have to go through intense periods of training, and then intense periods of rest.

When that sharp contrast is there between what you know you need to do and then relaxing, getting up, doing it and then relaxing, in good intervals, then you can sit back and see the result of your hard work. What contentment! You savour the satisfaction, fully. It's like some people say, having intense periods of work, rest and play like this is what builds character and stamina, and ultimately, satisfaction.

It's when we can achieve the optimum with that, then we're really doing well. We can then actually achieve a great deal. The whole of life is interval training for our next life. If we prepare our mind by always trying to think of the Lord, "*sa vai manah Kṛṣṇa padarvindayor vacamsi vaikuṇṭha gunana varnane*", like all the great emperors of this world, they meditated on Kṛṣṇa and achieved their ultimate destination. If we follow in their footsteps, we will also be able to achieve the highest result.

This is the process: one of developing our transcendental life and our transcendental body, which is there and it's something we can all achieve if we're prepared to work at it. That leads me nicely on to my next point.

The Spirituality of Meditation and Yoga

These things are important for a successful life. It's knowing what to meditate on, and what yoga to practice. So meditation is the mind thinking of something or someone. When we focus our thinking on one object, then we are meditating. But the question is, what should we meditate on to achieve the highest result?

That is described by Kṛṣṇa in the Bhaga-vad-gita, when He says, "man-mana bhava mad-bhakto mad-yaji mam namaskuru" (Bg.9.34) "Always think of Me, become My devotee, offer your obeisance unto Me, offer your homage unto Me, then surely you will come back to Me, to My abode in the spiritual world." So this is the ultimate result of all med-itation. The question is how to do that. And that is also described by Kṛṣṇa, when He says, «bhaktya mam abhijanati yavan yas casmi tat-tvatah.» "One can understand the Supreme Personality as He is only by devotional service.' (Bg.18.55)

In chapter six, text 47, Kṛṣṇa says, "Of all the yogis, the greatest yogi is one who is always thinking of Me." To try and get to that point where we're always thinking of Kṛṣṇa, we have to, first of all go through a process to do that. That is bhakti-yoga. There are nine steps to bhakti-yoga. The first is hearing. This is allowing ourselves to hear about the activities of Lord and the form of the Lord, and the benefits of chanting His holy name. By hearing the right things in life, we can actually achieve the highest result. Just by hearing, great things are achieved. When we first start, as babies, we hear, we learn to hear about how to do things, how to speak. So we imitate by hearing. By the process of hearing, we can develop the process of speaking.

By hearing ourselves first, and then listening to our inner voice of the soul, we become connected to the Supersoul, through these two things. The soul is sitting in the body and giving *life to the body. But it is getting its inspiration from the Supersoul. And depending on how little covering there is between the soul and the Supersoul, then the activity of what the soul does, is purified. So when the soul is connected to the Supersoul, by the hearing process, then he is able to chant very nicely.*

Chanting means, first of all, chanting the holy name of the Lord, or describing the activities of the Lord and His devotees. So, by hearing we can speak about speaking. Everyone is speaking something or other, but once we are connected to the Supersoul, then the speaking becomes transcendental, it becomes pure, it becomes effective. The chanting of the holy name of the Lord in the form of the Hare Kṛṣṇa mantra, («*Hare Kṛṣṇa, Hare Kṛṣṇa, Kṛṣṇa Kṛṣṇa, Hare Hare/ Hare Rāma, Hare Rāma, Rāma Rāma, Hare Hare*») is practiced by millions of people all over the world now. We can purify the mind by this transcendental process. We can purify the heart, so that the soul is connected to the Supersoul. By chanting the holy name of the Lord, one can be connected to the Supersoul. Just by listening to the chanting that we chant, we can be connected to the Supersoul.

OUR VAIKUṆṬHA PLANET

So this is the hearing and chanting process of bhakti yoga. And as already mentioned bhakti yoga itself comprises of a nine-fold process of yoga. There are other processes of yoga, which are eight-fold, or seven-fold or six- fold, like karma yoga, jnana yoga, raja yoga, and other yogas. But ultimately, the best yoga we can perform is the yoga of love or devotion to the Supreme Lord.

That is bhakti yoga. All the other yogas are included in bhakti-yoga, and one who has understood bhakti-yoga has already under-gone all the other yogas. So by hearing and chanting about the Supreme Lord, and first of all, hearing about His holy name, and then developing some taste for His qualities, «nama-rupa-guna-lila: His name, His form, His qualities and His activities.

We develop a taste for hearing and chant-ing about the name, fame, form, qualities, and pastimes and paraphernalia of the Lord in the association of devotees. Plus where He lives, His abode. Then we become very excited about life.

Because we are connected to the Supreme Lord, then, all our hearing and chanting becomes very blissful. This leads to trance, or samadhi as it is called, when we are fixed in remembering the Supreme Lord - that is the third stage of bhakti yoga- hearing, chanting and then remembering. That is what meditation really is. There are different degrees of meditation, where we will recollect the Supreme Lord, initially, and then sometimes we will forget.

Then gradually, when we become absorbed in thinking of the Supreme Lord and His devotees constantly and His activities, and His pastimes, and so on, it becomes deep meditation, and then we can come to the stage of realizing who we really are. And it's only then that we can actually perform our pure devotional service and our activities become in purified goodness.

We can then see everything as it is on the transcendental platform, above the three modes of material nature. Now, all the activities we do, may be conditioned by the modes of goodness, passion, or ignorance. Those three modes are always there. Sometimes one mode is more prominent, like goodness, and then passion and ignorance is less. Sometimes another mode is more prominent, like passion and then goodness and ignorance is less, since these modes are constantly changing, according to the mind and body, and what is happening in the world around us.

But once we become transcendentally situated above the three modes of material nature, by connecting to the Supreme Lord, through the process of hearing, chanting and remembering about His name, fame, form, qualities, pastimes, and His paraphernalia and His abode, then we become situated in samadhi, and all our activities become purified.

My Experience: My practice of bhakti-yoga of hearing, chanting and remembering the Lord has led me to expand that out to everything I hear, say and remember as something which relates to my relationship with Him.

Further, it has become possible to listen to people for a few hours, sometimes, relating their problems and then at the end them being completely rejuvenated and enlightened in their issues, without any further intervention from me.

Man Mohan Gupta

Spiritual practice has helped me to listen to people's problems very deeply and empathically to come to a satisfactory solution for all concerned.

So point 12 – what you need to note and work on is:

Become transcendentally situated above the three modes of material nature by -

> *12.1 Practicing your path faithfully and one day it will reap you enormous benefits*

> *12.2 Going by what the great masters have said and done and you can't go wrong*

> *12.3 Finding like-minded people to help you along the way.*

Then we're ready to perform some service to the Supreme Lord, which will help us and help everyone else. As Jesus said, «What profiteth a man if he gaineth the whole world at the loss of his own soul». We are all trying to serve ourselves or our families, communities, our nation, or the whole world. Ultimately, we have to see how effective this really is. Only if we have connected to the Supreme Lord will our activities be in purified goodness.

So we have to understand what is the nature of pure devotional service to the Supreme Lord, and that is only possible in disciplic succession, hearing from the pure devotee of the Lord, who can help us develop our taste for chanting, then remembering and then serving the Supreme Lord.

So that's the fourth stage, serving. Then beyond that is the transcendental rituals that we perform every day in the morning and evening, which try to develop our love for the Lord, ultimately, the fifth stage. Then there are prayers we can offer, and we offer reception of the Lord every morning into our heart.

When we do that, the Lord reciprocates with what we want to achieve in our life. This is a practical process that anyone can do, by gradually, developing a taste for it. This is bhakti yoga, and by this process of bhakti yoga, one can achieve the highest perfection of life, which Kṛṣṇa explains in Bhagavad-gita is to reach His eternal abode. The whole Bhagavad-gita is meant for action, it's not something sentimental in the mind. It's actually taking practical action under the direct guidance of the Lord.

Kṛṣṇa wanted Arjuna to take action against what had been done wrong against him. What people had done wrong against Arjuna and his brothers Kṛṣṇa wanted to explain to him that these people should not continue, they should not be allowed to continue. So that's why He encouraged Arjuna to fight. In this day and age, we can do the same thing by the process of bhakti yoga which is to speak something that's very nice.

By speaking, we are fighting against the modes of material nature. By saying something nice, we are actually producing a very good effect on the world. We don't have to physically fight with bullets and swords and weapons, and bombs and tridents and what have you… No…

Our greatest weapon is our words, speaking something, which is enlightening. That is what the Supreme Lord wants. Real peace comes about when we are peaceful ourself. And if for example, we have a conflict with someone else, if we are peaceful ourself, then it doesn't matter how bad it gets with the other person, we are always at peace with ourselves, thus there is no reaction. You see, there's no bad reaction when we are peaceful ourselves. So it is being situated in peace ourselves. That is wanted.

There's a nice verse, Kṛṣṇa says, peace comes

to the person who situated in Me.

❖ *bhoktaram yajna tapasam*
❖ *sarva-loka mahesvaram*
❖ *suhrdam sarva bhutanam*
❖ *jnatva mam santim rcchati (Bg.5.29)*

One who understands three things...

❖ *That Kṛṣṇa is the Supreme proprietor of everything.*
❖ *That He is the Supreme enjoyer of everything, and*
❖ *That He is the Supreme friend of all living entities*

then that person is situated in a peaceful condition of life always. He does not care for any external position and it doesn't matter what happens to him, people may try to knock him off his perch, but he will always remain peaceful. That's the position to be in life. It is to allow people to interact with you, and to carry on your activities, so that they are always peaceful.

There is no need for fighting with bombs and bullets. There is no need for that. But the real fighting is within, is making ourselves peaceful. And that's what we really need to do. We need to fight the enemy within. And if we can do that, and conquer our self, that's the greatest victory. All the great teachers and masters all over the world, they have all said the same thing.

They have said that the greatest victory a person can achieve in life is mastering over his own self. That is the process of bhakti yoga by reading about it in Bhagavad-gita. If not, if you don't want to read Bhagavad-gita, you can read the Koran, or you can read the Torah, or you can read the Bible, or you can read the Dharmapada .

Ultimately, these are all processes of achieving bhakti yoga, to engage the mind in thinking of the Supreme Lord, and developing love for Him. So when we do that, then we become very, very peaceful. All our desires are fulfilled when we are in that zone, in that mood, in that area in our life. That is possible to achieve for anyone. It is not something that is the preserve of a small few.

CHAPTER 7

Creating the Vaikuṇṭha Planet

Preaching Varnasrāma

By preaching Varnasrāma we can create a Vaikuṇṭha Planet and then Kṛṣṇa will be pleased and He will want to come down Himself or send His representative to rule over the planet. Sivarāma Svami explains very nicely in his book – *Varnasrāma Compendium that* Kṛṣṇa rules over all His Vaikuṇṭha planets through His system of Daiva Varnasrāma. So how can we presume to be above it? That would not be very sanguine. We have to follow the Lord's system systematically at every stage in our life, and then we will be successful, not otherwise.

OUR VAIKUNTHA PLANET

Srila Prabhupada has given us Kṛṣṇa. Now we have to give Kṛṣṇa to everyone in the form some activity they can do for Kṛṣṇa through this transcendental Daiva Varnasrāma Dharma Institution.

So, What Does Varnasrāma Actually Mean?

Varnasrāma means you have a head, arms, belly and legs, for your smooth day to day running of your life; for your family, for your society, for your country, and ultimately, for the UN.

Unless you are able to make a distinction between what your head is supposed to do, what your arms are supposed to do, or your belly is supposed to do and what your legs are supposed to do, unless you can distinguish between these functions, you will have complete and utter chaos. Nothing will work properly, and there will always be a form of madness prevailing. But as soon as the head is working nicely, then it can direct the arms, belly and legs to their natural normal function. Then the whole body will work very smoothly and properly for the satisfaction of the belly, which will then nourish every other part of the body.

That is a natural order, not something artificial or self-imposed from outside.

Then everyone will be pleased and eager to do their respective duties according to their natural ability and capacity. This will be according to their natural psychophysical makeup; it is a very simple thing. We just have to grasp it and then take full advantage of it.

The analogy of the human body is applied to the body, and extended to other members of your family, to the corporate body of your organization, to the body of your society, and ultimately to the body of the whole world. It all stems from getting our own body together by understanding how we work anatomically, and then reaching out beyond ourselves. Human society has to be divided into four divisions, for ease of understanding, to run smoothly, namely the *Brahmanas* – the thinking, literary, priestly class of people; the *Ksatriyas* – the ruling, fighting class of people to maintain law and order; the *Vaisyas* – the productive class of people who are the producers and purveyors of goods and services.

Finally, the Sudra class of people who actually make everything happen – the working class of people, the salt of the Earth. Not all classes of people want to labour hard for their livelihood, such as business people, politicians, teachers and advisors; it is simply working to your own capability, capacity and comfort, according to your natural inclination and qualification.

In short, a meritocracy as opposed to a democracy.

We might all be born equal, and certainly, we should all be given an opportunity to rise. In reality, not all of us are going to avail ourselves of that opportunity. However, we should all be allowed to participate in the smooth running of society, for the benefit of the whole. That is Varnasrāma. It ensures a full and productive life for everyone whilst on the planet and liberation when we leave. The idea of human life is to achieve our full potential by engaging in whatever activity we choose to do.

If we are to truly make progress in our lives, we must see for ourselves how we are developing ourselves on a daily, weekly, monthly and yearly basis, by associating with those who are on the path to progress in their lives. Birds of a feather flock together and in full flight formation traverse the skies to our ultimate destination.

Let's recap the steps.

1. *Take your medication.*

2. *Talk about your anxiety with others.*

3. *Smile until you are happy.*

4. *The philosophy or idea of not harming anyone or anything.*

5. *Take deep breaths of fresh air when you open a window, really.*

6. *The 7 Mini steps to get rid of your anxiety. By answering the following questions, you will write your own seven steps to get rid of your anxiety.*

   a. *Who have you spoken to about your anxiety?*

   b. *What have they said?*

   c. *How do you want to follow that up?*

d. *When do you plan on doing that?*

e. *Where will you be when you are free from your anxiety?*

f. *Why can't you get rid of it now?*

g. *Who, What, How, When, Where and Why can't you celebrate now?*

7. *Take a winter's hot drink to warm the heart*

8. *Write , Read , Listen*

   a. *Write a journal of your feelings to keep track of how you feel about the things going on in your life and identify what effects your anxiety.*

   b. *Read books that will distract you, teach you, and calm you when your experiencing anxiety.*

   c. *Listen to the calming music or sounds of Nature to relax your mind.*

9. *Take the time to reflect on what's happened in your life, and see how you can make something of it today.*

10. *Remember the Lord and He will inspire you, He will help your creative juices flow again. Even if you do not fully believe in him his magic will enhance your inspiration.*

11. *Know your body, Keep track of your sleeping patterns and see what works for you. If you get too much sleep it will affect you just a badly as if you get to little sleep. Not everyone needs the same amount of sleep and you need to work out how many hours of sleep has you the most relaxed and refreshed.*

12. *Become transcendentally situated above the three modes of material nature by –*

    a. *Practicing your path faithfully and one day it will reap you enormous benefits*

    b. *Going by what the great masters have said and done and you can't go wrong*

    c. *Finding like-minded people to help you along the way.*

OUR VAIKUNTHA PLANET

A *Brahmana* is someone who can teach anything. A *Sudra* is someone who can learn one specific art or craft and then work under someone to achieve perfection. A *Ksatriya* is one who can rule over the planet, if need be. A *Vaisya* is someone who can provide for everyone: money, food, and all the bare necessities of life. We must set up our cottage industries in Bhaktivedanta Manor village, immediately, taking cue from all global villages.

We must make provision for food, milk and water and cloth and simple building materials such as wood, metal, stone, clay, sand, cement, straw, concrete, bricks, and paper and ink. Nothing should go to waste, and, whatever there is, it must be fully utilized.

Krsna Caitanya Prabhu must grow some fruits and flowers as well as vegetables now, such as blackberries, raspberries, cherries, apples, pears, almonds, peaches, plums, gooseberries, rhubarb, and other things like fennel, fenugreek, radish, tomatoes, herbs and nuts and mint, coriander, thyme, basil, sage, lavender, and crops like wheat, barley and pulses, ginger, carrots, and turnips. We should have swans and peacocks by the lake.

A fool just says – I can't; a devotee says – Yes I can and does. That's all. So we must have our *patram, puspam, phalam, toyam, ausadhi* and *vanaspati* in our Bhaktivedanta Manor village as soon as possible. With *doodh, dahi, makkhan* and *ghee.* A little *Dhanvantari* Dhama at Bhaktivedanta Manor with roses, carnations and marigolds. As we know, the *Padma Purana* says:

jalaja nava-laksani
sthavara laksa-vimsati
krmayo rudra-sankhyakah
paksinam dasa-laksanam
trimsal-laksani pasavah
catur-laksani manusah

There are species of 900,000 aquatics, 2,000,000 *plants and trees*, 1,100,000 insects and reptiles, 1,000,000 birds, 3,000,000 animals, and 400,000 humans. Altogether, there are 8,400,000 different species of life. We want to create an area where we can grow 2 million different types of trees and plants or *sthavaras*.

We can accomplish this plan very easily in a small area. In London in Chelsea, for example, they have a wonderful medicine garden where they have about 5000 different herbs growing in a very small area. That's 5000 at the Chelsea Medicine Gardens, plus there is Kew Botanical Gardens in South West London. They have thousands of other species of plants and trees growing. If we work together, we can grow all 2 million trees and plants in a small area so that we have the full variety.

CHAPTER 8

How to Establish Varnasrāma in Nine Points

Establishing Varnasrāma Colleges.

So, from the outset, Srila Prabhupada has given us many instructions on how to do that, both individually and collectively to devotees and personal instructions that he gave to my father and myself. I would like to talk a little bit about that. I've already mentioned what is Varnasrāma in a little bit of detail and I would now like to mention how devotees all behaved and worked in the Daiva Varnasrāma Dharma Institution system, throughout the centuries.

Throughout the Satya Yuga, Treta Yuga, Kali Yuga and Dvapara Yuga.

OUR VAIKUṆṬHA PLANET

It is something that devotees have all practiced according to their ability and capacity. Then, I would like to say a little bit about how the Lord rules by Varnasrāma in other planets. The seventh part of my presentation will be on my personal journey. The eighth part is the prospectus for the Varnasrāma College. Finally, establishing our first Varnasrāma College in Europe at Bhaktivedanta Manor.

So those are all the headings and we will just go through them systematically.

First, Srila Prabhupada mentions Varnasrāma many times in his books; in particular, on the 12th and 13th of March 1974, Srila Prabhupada had some very specific conversations on the Varnasrāma morning walks (as they are famously called).

He asked us all to establish Varnasrāma Colleges, one with every Iskcon centre, just as we have technological colleges, agricultural colleges, and colleges of all sorts for trading people. So similarly, Srila Prabhupada has envisioned having Varnasrāma Colleges. In addition, there's a great deal of detail on that in *Hare Kṛṣṇa* Devi Dasi's book 'Srila Prabhu-pada Speaking about Varnasrāma', which was printed by the BBT, in 1999, and 1000 copies were printed. Every writer should try to read and understand the urgency of what Srila Prabhupada is saying here.

It is that important. The second part of this is that it is important to note that whatever the spiritual master says as his final instructions that is what the disciple should see as most important. Abhirāma Prabhu, who was Srila Prabhupada's nurse in 1977, about February 1977, I believe, asked Srila Prabhupada,

"What further do you have to achieve in your mission?"

"I've done 50% of my work, and the other 50% is to establish Varnasrāma."

"How will you do that, Srila Prabhupada?"

"I will go to Gita Nagari, sit there and teach how to live off the land."

So it is incumbent on all devotees, who are trying to establish Varnasrāma to teach people how to live off the land, by living off the land themselves. That is the ideal position of

Varnasrāma. So a Varnasrāma College will teach people how to grow your own food, milk your own cows, weave your own cloth, build your own shelter, produce everything you need, and use everything you produce.

That is the idea of a Varnasrāma College. Srila Prabhupada also says that a *Brahmana* is someone who can teach any subject and a *Sudra* is someone who can learn to serve under his direction. So this is our position. Further, if we look at what Srila Prabhupada has said about Varnasrāma in the *Srimad Bhagavatam*, in his latter days, when he was translating right to the very end on Canto 10, chapter 13, text 53, Srila Prabhupada is again talking about how to establish Varnasrāma in order to raise people to *Sattva Guna* or the mode of goodness. It is only when people are in the mode of goodness that we can actually think about becoming Kṛṣṇa conscious. The whole process of Varnasrāma is to raise people to the platform of goodness. If we can do that, then we can actually establish pure goodness after that. In addition, as devotees, we have to practice that also.

Man Mohan Gupta

Kṛṣṇa Consciousness

We see that when we first come to Kṛṣṇa consciousness, we may not be in pure goodness. Therefore, gradually by the process of following our natural propensity in Kṛṣṇa consciousness, we can derive the highest benefit and that means following our psychophysical nature to do the ultimate good and reach the ultimate destination.

It is interesting to note that the whole Kṛṣṇa consciousness movement is based on chanting, dancing and feasting. That is *sankirtana:* book distribution, *prasadam* distribution, and chanting the holy name of the Lord. Those are the first steps to creating good people who will actually come forward to take initiation and become serious about doing good for others in the world. So there is the initiation system in our movement, followed by establishing temples, a place where people can stay, and practice and associate with one another so that we can actually develop pure love of God.

The temples are an essential part of the plan to establish a *Vaikuṇṭha* Planet. But ultimately, we must be living a simple life and high thinking:

Varnasrāma. Those four things constitute Srila Prabhupada's full mission.

In the *Rathayatra* of 1976 in New York, Srila Prabhupada mentions something very interesting in his lecture, which was a ticker tape affair, with thousands of people coming out on the streets, it being the greatest *Rathayatra* of all time. Srila Prabhupada was very pleased and gave a wonderful lecture at that time. There, Srila Prabhupada says that if we carry on these festivals in this way, one day, the whole planet will become like *Vaikuṇṭha*. So, this is our aim through our *sankirtana,* through our initiation, through our temple construction projects.

Ultimately, by establishing Varnasrāma, we are to create a *Vaikuṇṭha* planet. That is something for which we all striving. It is not an impossible dream. It is just working together, and seeing how we can make it happen. What comes to mind is the final one of many instructions Srila Prabhupada gave to my father, in 1976 on Sunday July 26th when Srila Prabhupada came to our house and stayed for many hours.

Man Mohan Gupta

At one point, my father asked Srila Prabhupada – what service he could render further and Srila Prabhupada said at that time – 'please establish Daiva Varnasrāma Dharma by practical example'. So my father was previously a *brahmacari* and then at that time a *grhastha*, and shortly after that, he became a *vanaprastha*. **Then after my mother passed away, he took sannyasa.** So he followed the four *asrāmas* as one should. And he instructed his sons and everyone he met on to how to lead a practical life in Kṛṣṇa consciousness, ultimately for one's own benefit and for the benefit of others, and thus do something nice for the planet. So that is the way of the mahajanas: *mahajano gatena sa panthah.*

In *Vrndavana in* 2011, the devotees made a very nice film of how Srila Prabhupada's mission in Varnasrāma was to be executed. So that film, I do not know if it is on YouTube or if it is available. But it would be helpful for every devotee to see how other devotees all over the planet, are working to establish Srila Prabhupada's Varnasrāma mission, in particular, our GBC Minister for Daiva Varnasrāma, His Holiness Bhakti Raghava Svami, who has done the world-wide community of devotees real sterling service in raising awareness on the importance of Varnasrama for many years together now. If we all simply just gather under his lotus feet and take instruction from him, that will bring about the real change in consciousness that we are all looking for in our movement.

I am now ready to record the fourth part of my book. First, talking a little bit about the devotees in Varnasrama, and then secondly my two Vyasa Puja offerings to Srila Prabhupada this year.

Thirdly, how, by Kṛṣṇa's mercy, we are now establishing a Varnasrama College at Bhaktivedanta Manor, with Akhandadhi Prabhu appointed as the Director of the Varnasrama College there now. Finally, some poems I wrote on 1 August 2019, and 7 August 2019 in glorification of Sri Sri Radha Londonisvara's 50th Anniversary Installation ceremony.

The devotees in Varnasrama are unlimited in number, since all devotees of Kṛṣṇa work under the Daiva Varnasrama Dharma Institution. I have chosen a few examples, just to illustrate what I mean. First of all, Sudama

Vipra, he was a brahmana, and he practiced all the principles of brahmanical life and achieved the highest perfection as Krsna's dear friend.

Arjuna was a ksatriya. He fought on behalf of the Lord on the Battlefield of Kuruksetra and became successful, again, as one of Krsna's dearmost friends. Then there was Nanda Maharaja, who was a vaisya and he was Krsna's foster father. He nurtured Krsna as a baby. He is glorious as a vaisya, taking care of Krsna and the cows.

Finally, we have Sabri, who is a sudrani in Lord Rāmacandra's time. She stayed in her status as a lower class person, but she achieved the highest perfection by pleasing Lord Rāmacandra. So the point is, all these devotees are in a different status and strata of society, but, they all achieved the highest perfection of life, just by executing the duties in their varna or particular order of society.

So, this is how we can achieve perfection by fulfilling our duties in our particular status, according to varna and asrāma that is what Krsna wants of us. Bhakti-yoga, as we know is the nine fold process of yoga – sravanam, kirtanam, visnu smaranam, pada-sevanam, arcanam, vandanam, dasyam, sakhyam, atma-nivedanam.

Each of these nine processes have a devotee who has achieved perfection by executing devotional service, according to his varna and asrama, for example, Maharaja Pariksit heard from Sukadeva Gosvami recite the Srimad Bhagavatam. Just by listening to Srimad Bhagavatam, as a king, he was a ksatriya, but by the process of listening about Krsna, he achieved the highest perfection.

Sukadeva Gosvami himself was a devotee of Krsna, and he explains throughout the Srimad Bhagavatam how Varnasrama is so important for everyone to follow. In particular, in the 7th canto, there is a huge description of how Varnasrama is so important, and he quotes Narada Muni, on explaining how it is to be unfolded on this planet.

So, all these great devotees, they explain that Varnasrama is so important, and further, we see the great Vaishnava emperors of this world – *Maharaja Ambarisa, Maharaja Yudhisthira,*

Man Mohan Gupta

Maharaja Pariksit, Maharaja Janmejaya, - there is so many great kings who ruled over the whole planet- just by executing their varna and asrāma perfectly they achieved the highest perfection of life.

This is the point about this principle that if we follow in the footsteps of the great acaryas, the great teachers, the great saints, the great royal kings, then we too will achieve the highest perfection. Now, His Holiness Bhakti Raghava Svami have written about this at length. Madhava Priya Devi Dasi and Krṣṇa Asraya Prabhus, wrote a book called 'Varnasrāma College Now', which you may like to read. I helped to edit it a few years ago.

We have to see how we can establish Varnasrāma, through a Varnasrāma College with every ISKCON centre. Another example is Jadabharata, he was a great devotee of the Lord. But later on, he took on the role of a brahmana and instructed Maharaja Rahugana, the emperor of the whole world.

So we can see that devotees are always ready to take on duties relating to both varna and asrāma for the benefit of all mankind. They fully understand that they are not bound by the rules and regulations of the Varnasrāma system, but at the same time, they don't neglect it, because they have realized the whole organisational structure of human society is meant for the pleasure of the Lord and all living entities.

There must be this hierarchy; and it is a transcendental hierarchy because it starts from the feet of the Lord. We pray to the Lord, and we pray to spiritual master every morning: the only we can execute pure devotional service is by bowing down at Their lotus feet and thus getting a drop of Their unlimited mercy. This is the only way to perfection, by pleasing the spiritual master through his lotus feet, and then we can actually achieve the highest perfection.

So the lowest strata of our society are not neglected because of Varnasrāma. Everyone can participate in it, whatever level they're at. Moreover, we see in the modern times, that one devotee, Tulsi Gabbard, she is making great progress in trying to head up the United States government. This is very much wanted in our society today, when devotees actually take the lead in helping society by taking on prominent positions. Then, almost overnight, there will be peace on the planet.

Therefore, this is what is wanted. *This is what Varnasrāma will achieve.* The perfection of your education is when you can link it to the Supreme Lord and glorify His name, fame, form, qualities, pastimes, devotees and paraphernalia to the best of your ability. Nothing short of this qualifies for perfection.

So my idea of producing more books is to take whatever subjects I have studied at school, college and university and show how each of them can be dovetailed in the Lord's service and so give life to otherwise dead matter. So going through each of my true loves in chronological order they will be teaching maths, physics, samskrta, music, art, and learning to write. These are all things that will be taught in my Varnasrāma College.

For more details, subscribe to our website in order to keep up with the latest training and developments. www.daivalimited.com

CHAPTER 9

Vyasa Puja Offerings

I would like to share the two Vyasa puja offerings that I made to Srila Prabhupada this year on Thursday, the 1st of August 2019, and Saturday, the 24th of August 2019, Srila Prabhupada's Appearance Day at Bhaktivedanta Manor, something that all the devotees heartily enjoyed.

I would like to say at this point that for many years I had wanted to make these offerings, and each year I would get more and more anxious about when I would be allowed to present them on the day and each year I would come away more and more distraught, but somehow or other, this year I was allowed to present my thoughts without interruption and they were graciously received. So all was well that ended well…

But now the real work begins

The First Offering

So the first piece was written for the ISK-CON London Community Vyasa Puja Offerings Compilation book.

❖ *Om ajnana timirandasya jnananjana salakaya*

❖ *Caksur unmilitam yena tasmai sri gurave namah*

I was born in the darkness of ignorance, but my spiritual master opened my eyes with the torchlight of knowledge, and thus I offer my respectful obeisances unto him at his divine lotus feet.

It is very wonderful to be given this opportunity to glorify you once again, Srila Prabhupada, before the erudite assembly of esteemed Vaishnava devotees of the Lord, guests, on-lookers, and everyone else on this day, Thursday the 1st of August 2019, just 23 days before your actual appearance day, on Saturday the 24th of August 2019 here in London, where the sun appears to be shining and hiding under some dark clouds at the same time. A place where the empire rose, so great, that the sun never set and now so small that the sun never seems to rise. If we simply convince people to eat Kṛṣṇa prasadam, that alone will encourage the sun god to appear more often.

And as you often said, what is the difficulty in understanding that. You are always looking out for the welfare of everyone on the planet, and in particular those living in England and London. You set out a 5-point plan for the UK.

- ❖ First of all, you said to distribute a set of your books in every home.

- ❖ Secondly, to build a temple in the Regent's Park.

- ❖ Three, 10 temples in London.

- ❖ Four, theatre for the British public, and

- ❖ Five, the British Empire of Kṛṣṇa Consciousness.

OUR VAIKUṆṬHA PLANET

So it will be. Just recently on March 19th 2019, I determined to meet some billionaires Gopichand Hinduja and Anil Agrawal at our temple at 10 Soho Street, London, which I did and in the process I felt the need to spend more time with the devotees there.

And so for the next 37 days I spent up to 10 hours a day sitting in reception encouraging all the devotees and guests with your above 5-point plan. Whilst there, one devotee asked me, *"What personal association did you have with Srila Prabhupada?"* I replied, *"Very little. I was only a child of 10 years of age. But I recall nine times when Srila Prabhupada personally spoke to me during his manifest presence here."* I then wrote down those nine times and showed them to the devotee. These are as follows:

❖ One: 'So long as you are with your father everything will be all right.' This is something Srila Prabhupada said to me at Bhaktivedanta Manor in 1973.

❖ Two: Srila Prabhupada said, 'Continue your education and become Kṛṣṇa conscious.' Again, this was at the Manor in 1973.

❖ Three: 'Have at least two rounds.' This was in relation to neck beads at the Manor again in 1973.

❖ Four: 'Your father has not taught you?' This is in relation to chanting gayatri when I was receiving gayatri initiation at the Manor in 1973.

❖ Five: 'Where is your father?' Srila Prabhupada rolled down the window to his car whilst sitting in the back seat of a big car at Orly Airport in Paris in 1973. I was standing a little way to the side and he beckoned to me and asked me where is my father was. I was very afraid of approaching Srila Prabhupada and I didn't know what to say. Srila Prabhupada was not very happy because I didn't say very much. I was always very afraid.

❖ Six: 'You have more?' This was at The ISKCON Paris temple in 1973, in relation to an Ekadasi feast I cooked for Srila Prabhupada. It was something that Srila Prabhupada really enjoyed. He asked me if I had more.

❖ Seven: And then he ordered me 'Bring more' to some potato halva I had made, together with some grated potato chivra and peanuts and sultanas, and some other things. Srila Prabhupada really enjoyed it.

❖ Eight: 'Vibhāgaśaḥ!' When I was with my whole family, 5 of us, my father, my mother, my 2 brothers and myself, we visited Srila Prabhupada at the Manor in 1973 and my father kept pressing me to say a verse from Bhagavad-gita in front of Srila Prabhupada. I was very shy and I didn't want to say anything. But then my father pressed me more. And so in the end I finally relented and blurted out Chapter 4 verse 13 from Bhagavad-gita: *cātur-varṇyaṁ mayā sṛṣṭaṁ guṇa-karma-vibhāgaśa.*

❖ As soon as I said, vibhāgaśa, Srila Prabhupada corrected me and said vibhāgaśaḥ! That is with the visarga ending. I remember that very clearly. I should always remember to put the visarga at the end of every verse that has it.

And then finally,

❖ Nine: 'What is this?' In relation to some uncooked rice, soggy chapattis and mud dahl that I cooked for Srila Prabhupada, again at the Manor in 1973. Srila Prabhupada was not very happy, but somehow or other,

❖ by his unlimited mercy, he still ate it. He asked Srutakirti Prabhu, his servant, what was going on and said he should have supervised the boy. I was 14 at the time. I realized that Srila Prabhupada is a great ocean of mercy.

I beg to be forgiven
for all my offences.

The Second Offering

Now I would like to read the Vyasa Puja offering that I read out on Saturday the 24th of August 2019 at the Bhaktivedanta Manor before the assembled devotees and guests. I first of all started by mentioning one instruction that Srila Prabhupada gave me, which was to 'Continue your education and become Kṛṣṇa conscious' and so in that light and vein, I have decided to write a book on Varnasrāma, which glorifies my mother, my father, my spiritual master, my brothers, and all my Godbrothers and -sisters, which will set the tone for the next 50 years of our movement. In doing that, I would simply be learning to write nicely. The real need for our movement is learning how to read, how to write and how to do arithmetic in Kṛṣṇa consciousness.

Education, Education, Education.

Real education is becoming free from the pangs of birth, death, old age and disease. That is our prime duty. Unless we become free from the three modes of material nature, and we are transcendentally situated, there is no question of understanding who we are, where we have come from and where we are going. All our hopes for perfection will remain incomplete, unless we master the secret of Kṛṣṇa consciousness, which is

Sa vai manah Kṛṣṇa padarvindayor vacamsi vaikuṇṭha gunanavarnane

Unless we fix our mind at the lotus feet of Kṛṣṇa, whilst we are here on this planet, we will not be able to go back to the spiritual world. Therefore, learning how to always think of Kṛṣṇa, in everything we do, in our dealings with other devotees, in our service to the Lord, in how to deal with our health, in how to carry out the order of the spiritual master perfectly, and in all other matters, the prime factor is fixing our mind on Kṛṣṇa's lotus feet.

* ❖ *man-mana bhava mad-bhakto*
* ❖ *mad-yaji mam namaskuru*

Kṛṣṇa actually says this twice in Bhaga-vad-gita (9.34) and (18.65). So, if we agree to do that, then we will be successful. We can go on with our sankirtana, distributing books, chanting the holy name, and distributing pras-adam. We can go on initiating more and more people into Kṛṣṇa consciousness. We can go on building more and more temples all over the world. But our prime duty is to fix our mind on Kṛṣṇa's lotus feet. And we will not be able to do that, unless we find the perfect means to execute the order of the bona-fide spiritual master.

OUR VAIKUṆṬHA PLANET

That is His Divine Grace A.C. Bhaktivedanta Svami Srila Prabhupada. Srila Prabhupada repeatedly emphasized the need for dividing society up into four divisions – brahmanas, ksatriyas, vaisyas and sudras. Without these four divisions, we are simply living in a dog society, not a God society. Sri Caitanya Mahaprabhu revealed three of His most wonderful forms to Murari Gupta, who wrote kadacas on the early life of the Lord and worked as a physician: The Lord's Caturbhuja form, the Lord's *maha- prakasa* form of Lord Rāmacandra and the Lord's Varaha-murti form. The Lord was so pleased with Murari Gupta, that he revealed these forms all to him.

We, incidentally, are coming in Murari Gupta's line as Kedarnath Gupta, Ksirodakasayi Viṣṇu Maharaja, Kamla Gupta, Kirti Ma Devi Dasi, Rajendra Gupta or Radha Mohan Gupta, Caturbhuja Prabhu, Man Mohan Gupta – myself, Kāraṇodakaśāyī Viṣṇu Dāsa Adhikārī and Madan Mohan Gupta, Sandipani Muni Prabhu. The Lord then revealed to Murari Gupta, his eternal form as Hanuman, the greatest servant of Lord Rāmacandra.

This was all because Murari Gupta established Daiva Varnasrāma Dharma by practical example, as a physician, using whatever he earned to spread Daiva Varnasrāma Dharma. So, the real need for our world at the present time is establishing Varnasrāma, and by that, I mean Varnasrāma Colleges. Srila Prabhupada gave his famous Varnasrāma morning walk conversations in Mayapur on March 12th and March 13th 1974, where he said we must have one Varnasrāma College with every Iskcon centre. Without that our Kṛṣṇa consciousness movement cannot progress on very well. The extent to which we neglect this instruction, the greater we go down as a society and take everyone else with it. The order of the spiritual master is our life and soul, so we must find the means to execute it perfectly.

If we agree to abide by the transcendental order of the spiritual master, we immediately flourish and come back to life again. Therefore, I say, without establishing Varnasrāma Colleges, with each ISKCON centre today, we will not be able to maintain our pure preaching spirit, to the heads of state, to the kings and queens of this world, to the next generation of devotees and to society at large. Thank you very much.

After My Offerings

The next part is how, after giving this talk, I learnt the devotees agreed to have our first Varnasrāma College in Europe at Bhaktivedanta Manor in the newly constructed building there called the Haveli. So this is a victory for common sense as I wrote a paper on establishing a Varnasrāma College in 2012 and distributed to all the devotees at the time.

Better late than never.In that paper, I laid out 40 founding principles for a Varnasrāma College. I will just mention them here quickly.

- ❖ *A Varnasrāma College will bring about global peace. This is something Srila Prabhupada said, and it is quoted in Siksamrta on Varnasrāma.*

- ❖ *A Varnasrāma College will bring about full employment.*

- ❖ *A Varnasrāma College will prove that Kṛṣṇa is the Supreme Personality of Godhead by all the 2000 fields of endeavour taught in schools, colleges, gurukulas, universities and all other training and educational institutions, globally.*

❖ *A Varnasrāma College will implement the work of the Bhaktivedanta Institute by sharing consciousness within the sciences with all of our scientists and educationalists.*

❖ *A Varnasrāma College will teach Bhakti-sastri, Bhakti-vaibhava, Bhaktivedanta and Bhakti-sarvabhauma. And PhDB which is Dr. of Bhagavata Philosophy which Srila Prabhupada asked us to implement by connecting with the University of Calcutta and have an ISKCON Bhagavata College in Mayapura. So that is there.*

❖ *A Varnasrāma College will provide education and training for all 265 heads of state.*

❖ *A Varnasrāma College will give direction to the United Nations Secretary-General: how to adopt one book – Bhagavad-gita; how to worship one*

God – Lord Sri Kṛṣṇa; how to chant one mantra – Hare Kṛṣṇa, Hare Kṛṣṇa, Kṛṣṇa Kṛṣṇa, Hare Hare/ Hare Rāma, Hare Rāma, Rāma Rāma, Hare Hare;

❖ *how to adopt one work – service to the Supreme Personality of Godhead; and how to establish one language - Samskrta deva-bhasa for the whole world, a franca lingua and*

❖ *To have, as a result, one world government and one world Emperor to rule over the whole planet. This is going to be possible by establishing Varnasrāma Colleges all over the world.*

❖ *A Varnasrāma College will teach us how to grow our own food, how to milk our own cows, how to weave our own cloth, how to build our own shelter, how to produce everything we need, and how to use everything we produce.*

❖ *Ten, A Varnasrāma College will teach simple living and high thinking by producing only what we need and using everything that we produce.*

❖ *Eleven, A Varnasrāma College will teach all the 64 Vedic arts and sciences.*

❖ *Twelve, A Varnasrāma College will not be simply an educational institution, but also a social, cultural, political, entrepreneurial, and practical operational institution based on pure spiritual life.*

❖ *A Varnasrāma College will teach the 14 books of Vedic knowledge, which are:*

    ❑ *The 4 Vedas:–*

        ✦ *Rg-veda*

        ✦ *Sama-veda*

        ✦ *Yajur-veda*

        ✦ *Atharva-veda*

    ❑ *The 6 Vedangas :–*

        ✦ *Siksa-**phonetics or pronunciation***

        ✦ *Chanda - **meter poetry***

        ✦ *Nirukti – **dictionary***

OUR VAIKUṆṬHA PLANET

- ✦ *Jyotisa - astronomy and astrology*

- ✦ *Kalpa - deity worship, yajnas and samskaras, and*

- ✦ *Vyakarana – grammar*

❑ *Then the 4 Upangas ;-*

- ✦ *The Dharma Sastras – including Canakya Pandita's Niti Sastra and Manu Samhita or the Vedic Book of Law.*

- ✦ *Vedanta - philosophy*

- ✦ *Nyaya - logic*

- ✦ *Purana – history, including the Itihasas which are the Rāmayana and the Mahabharata*

  - ○ *Then the Vedic sciences as taught in the Upa-Puranas, namely:-*

  - ○ *Ayurveda – medicine*

  - ○ *Gandharva-veda – performing arts*

- ○ *Sthapya-veda – vastu or the science of sacred space*

- ○ *Dhanur-veda – military science.*

❖ *A Varnasrāma College will teach Pancaratrika viddhi and Bhagavata viddhi.*

❖ *A Varnasrāma College will teach the* srutis *- theoretical knowledge. Sruti refers to spiritual and to transcendental knowledge that is heard, and* smrti *refers to practical knowledge that is remembered and is applicable and can be put into practice.*

❖ *The smrtis encompass all material arts and sciences needed for functioning properly while living in this material world.*

❖ *In any science, a theory is proven by its application. Therefore, the smrtis are evidence, the applications demonstrating the srutis of the theoretical basis for all knowledge.*

❖ *A Varnasrāma College will teach how to come back to the countryside, stay in your village, cultivate your soil, milk your cows and chant Hare Kṛṣṇa.*

❖ *A Varnasrāma College will teach Samskrta, Bengali, English and one's mother tongue at the very least.*

❖ *A Varnasrāma College with teach all soft technologies found in villages, globally.*

❖ *A Varnasrāma College will be attached to each ISKCON center, or temple globally and there will be 1008 such Varnasrāma Colleges.*

❖ *A Varnasrāma College will be funded from the 4 main sources:*

❑ **Public sector** - *which includes the United Nations, central governments, local governments, and other agencies.*

❑ **Private sector** - *multi-national companies and businesses.*

❑ **Voluntary sector** – *charities, trusts and foundations, and*

❑ **Individual sponsorships and donations.**

❖ *A Varnasrāma College will establish Vedic culture and civilization, globally.*

❖ *A Varnasrāma College will teach sambandha jnana, abhideya jnana and prayojana jnana.*

❖ *A Varnasrāma College with teach how to bring all ISKCON farms up to date, and relevant to the present time with the view to accommodating any number of people who want to stay there.*

❖ *A Varnasrāma College will teach how to divide society into four social orders, namely, Brahmanas, Ksatriyas, Vaisyas and Sudras and four spiritual orders – Brahmacaris, Grhasthas, Vanaprasthas and Sannyasis.*

❖ *A Varnasrāma College will incorporates all Bhakti Life courses and those undertaken by all ISKCON educational institutions, such as Bhaktivedanta College, VIHE, MIHE, and Bhaktivedanta Academy and Rupanuga Vedic college, the ISKCON Youth Foundation, Vaikuṇṭha players and so on. In this way, a Varnasrāma College will seek to converge and unite organizations, communities and countries in order to create harmony and stability everywhere.*

❖ *A Varnasrāma College will be based on tertiary level of education, along the lines of the Kṛṣṇa Avanti primary and secondary system of education. At the heart will be the ISKCON temple and around the periphery will be the Varnasrāma College.*

❖ *A Varnasrāma College will offer across-the-spectrum courses from fully residential to day-only.*

❖ *A Varnasrāma College will be for 10 years of age and upwards, both for men and women to learn and teach all cottage industries, as discovered at our present ISKCON communities, such as New Vrndavana in West Virginia and Spanish Folk in Utah.*

❖ *Each Varnasrāma College will have a purpose built temple, if one does not already exist, with all the surrounding land and property belonging to the presiding Deity, along the lines of the system of Sri Jagannatha Puri in India.*

❖ *A Varnasrāma College will take our Kṛṣṇa consciousness movement into its second phase based on land, cows, grhasthas, and Varnasrāma-dharma.*

❖ *A Varnasrāma College will cater for a community within a 10 miles radius. Typically if it is 1,000 miles from John O'Groats to Land's End, there will be approximately 50 communities, diagonally, and similarly worked out crossways as appropriate.*

❖ *A Varnasrāma College will, in this way, be the focus for a Varnasrāma Village or a Vrndavana Village, with appropriate divisions of Brahmanas, Ksatriyas, Vaisyas and Sudras. Candalas and others will live outside the village.*

❖ *A Varnasrāma College would form the basis for the Daiva Varnasrāma Dharma Institution, which will be the means to create a Vaikuṇṭha Planet.*

❖ *A Varnasrāma College is meant for making a person self-sufficient, self-sustained and self-realized by developing all 50 qualities of a jiva tattva and thus attain his full potential in one lifetime.*

❖ *A Varnasrāma College will form as result of the purity of the chanting of the Holy name and proof of the efficacy and efficiency of the sankirtana movement of Lord Caitanya Mahaprabhu and, thus, usher in another wave of the Golden period.*

❖ *A Varnasrāma College will have at its core, all the books of His Divine Grace A.C. Bhaktivedanta Swami Srila Prabhupada, and his disciples and followers to take direction for its philosophy, management and administration, its funding and its application and operation.*

❖ *A Varnasrāma College will have the following: -*

    ❑ *Brahmanas - for studying and teaching, fire sacrifices, deity worship and samskaras.*

    ❑ *Ksatriyas - for management, administration, law and order.*

    ❑ *Vaisyas - for cow protection, agriculture, horticulture, permaculture, trade, commerce and banking.*

    ❑ *Sudras - for manufacturing all items of arts and crafts under cottage industries and services, such as performing kirtana and theatre.*

❖ *A Varnasrāma College's purpose is to create a God-centred society, globally.*

❖ *A Varnasrāma College will teach how to minimize and downsize in the cities by having city farms and community gardens.*

❖ *A Varnasrāma College will teach the science of Kṛṣṇa and devotional service.*

OUR VAIKUṆṬHA PLANET

This was written on Saturday 19th April 2012 and distributed to all the devotees shortly afterwards. These 40 points or principles are something that I have been very anxious to implement since 2012, after coming back from Mayapura in 2011 and 2012, but not had an opportunity to air them as freely as now. So, this is a cathartic release for me.

For details about each point and how it has affected me as well as how it can help you with your Anxiety, Please see the website for the training and bonus material.

CHAPTER 10

My Poems

I would like to share with you a few poems I wrote. One on the 1st of August 2019 and two others on the Wednesday, the 7th of August 2019.

College-Temple-Farm-Prayer

Arise! O morning dew on August day,

To meet their Lordships to work and play

To meet their Lordships to work and play

Arise! O morning dew on August day.

I know not how to work and play

To work and play,

OUR VAIKUṆṬHA PLANET

I know not how to work and play.

For You, my dear Kṛṣṇa, have stolen my heart,

Please return me my heart

So that I may work and play

And work and play.

*How else will You come to live in that sweeter
than sweeter abode of Yours, my Lord?*

In the gardens and groves of Regents' Park

In the midst of fountains, lakes, and waterfalls.

*The swans await You, my Lord, glancing here
and there in ever increasing anxiety.*

Another poem I wrote was on Wednesday,
the 7th of August 2019.

Prayer in Separation

*O my Lord and Master, friend of the poor,
when will you allow me to serve you again?*

With crips potato halva,

Man Mohan Gupta

And fried peanuts and roasted sultanas

And grated potatoes together with chaunced sesame seeds and spices, sugar and salt and lemon and black pepper,

And soft sweet cheese made of milk and sugar with almonds, sultanas and dessicated coconut.

When, O when, will I have another chance to cook you proper dahl soup, sweet flavoured rice and full-blown chapattis?

When, O when, will I be allowed to serve you again in some more menial way for your great pleasure and delight?

When, O when, will I be allowed to add another mustard seed to the bag of mustard seeds you're collecting for the Lord?

When, O when, will we all unite again to serve you once again to save the fallen condition souls?

When, O when, will Lord Gauranga once again appear in all His paintings and fill the hearts of the fallen condition souls with His pure love and Bhakti.

May that day come sooner than I think.

OUR VAIKUṆṬHA PLANET

A poem for Sri Sri Radha Londonisvara on behalf of Caturbhuja Prabhu, who asked me to write this on Wednesday, the 7th of August 2019.

To My Heart's Delight

O Moon-faced One with beautiful cheeks,

Let me kiss You, to delight 'n peaks.

You stand so still, You are ever moving,

You stand so still, but are ever staring.

In the cockles of my heart,

You appear so bright,

With Your consort, my heart's delight.

When O when, my dear Kṛṣṇa, will You quench my thirst?

To build You a place as big as Buckingham Palace,

Not far from a place You call Primrose Hill.

Next to a lake, canal, waterfall and fountain

Man Mohan Gupta

For the whole world to see Your simple beauty,
Among the stars, grass and men of duty.

There was a little boy called Mo

There was a little boy called Mo,
Who didn't want to play in the snow.
When asked why,
He didn't reply.

He just wanted to play dumb,
So, he pulled out his thumb.
Which was now a lump,
So, he was down in the dump.

But could not say,
Why he could not play.
All because he was depressed.
'What is the matter, son', his father asked?
'I want to be with God',
His mother gave the nod
And then they both departed.

OUR VAIKUNṬHA PLANET

The boy left to his devices,
Now gave up his vices.

Spent all his time thinking of God,
Until the time came to do something.
He decided to write, to write to the world.
And before he knew it, he had done it.

The whole world was quiet and peaceful.
And he could now play in the snow to his
heart's delight.
A ship so tight.

CHAPTER 11

A Few Words from the Heart.

Finally, I would like to say, thank you all my God-brothers and -sisters who are working very hard to establish Varnasrāma and Varnasrāma Colleges everywhere. In particular, Bhakti Raghava Svami, who is the Minister for Daiva Varnasrāma Dharma in the Governing Body Commission of the International Society for Kṛṣṇa Consciousness.

It is very heartening to see the Vedic eco-village that he has established just near Vancouver in Canada. And the wonderful Varnasrāma place that he has formulated in Hebri, South India, together with Radhanatha Maharaja's Govardhana eco-village, near Pune.

OUR VAIKUṆṬHA PLANET

Gradually, we can see that devotees are seeing the importance of Varṇasrāma everywhere. If we can, as Lokanatha Maharaja has asked me to do, keep talking about it and virtually everyone will become very enthused and realise its great importance. Moreover, of course, Sivarāma Svami has established the very nice Kṛṣṇa Valley in Hungary.

My God-brother, Langaganesa Prabhu writes of being completely enthused with his project in New Talavana, in Mississippi. In addition, my God-sister, Asta-sakhi is planning something very soon. So it is wonderful, that these projects are going on. We need to keep moving forward, just as we meant to start with everything on Varṇasrāma. Then for sure, we will get Srila Prabhupada's full mercy.

Next part, the secret to becoming a writer is simply to write, read and write, read and write. Anything you read, write about it straight away. Then you become a living machine, a living organism, a thriving, surviving, hiving machine. Then you don't end up becoming a dead sponge or a parasite on society.

Man Mohan Gupta

Life is not just about reading; it's about writing too and good writing at that. As soon as you practice reading, start writing too. Practice makes perfect writing. After 60 years, I realized the best things in life come when you create your own. For 60 years, I simply sponged, copied, and absorbed the world. Now for the next 60 years, I intend to create my own. When you discover what you didn't know before, that is pure joy.

I had 50 years of solitary confinement that was self-imposed. You are in the world, but not of it. Writing now has released me from solitary confinement; I can now at least talk. Something people for 60 years had told me not to do.. This indeed is a defining moment for me, one that will change my life for good. I had 10 O-levels, 5 A-levels and a degree from Oxford, and I had lived out over 30 years of my life after that.

However, the sheer exuberance of being able to express myself for the first time in my life was out of this world. Writing really is the real business. *The 50 years of confinement has been a blessing.* It has allowed me to see through a very sharp laser focus, a world that will be, rather than what has been. When you stand on this platform of truth, fake news is decimated. You begin to realize, why the world is so silent. It is just Kṛṣṇa's mercy.

Fact is stranger than fiction and all fiction is based on fact. If you can think it, it is probably happening in some universe or other, at some time or another in another place. However, reality is what is happening to you at this moment in time and where your thoughts are now. *sa vai manah Kṛṣṇa padarvindayor vacamsi vaikuṇṭha gunana varnane*

Kṛṣṇa and Kṛṣṇa's devotees and their activities are the only reality. I have written 150 notebooks, journals and diaries over the last 13 years. However, this is my first published book.

I hope you enjoyed it. There is a lot to be said for the slow period of gestation. The Lord does everything in His own time, we in ours. Hence, it makes sense to try to go with the flow of nature, the Lord's nature, and so make our life a success.

Swimming upstream is not wanted. Everything that happens in a devotee's life is all to the good. We just have to accept that the Lord knows best. My maths, Samskrta and money books are going to have to wait till later. For now, it is just concentrating on Vaikuṇṭha and Varnasrāma, that's all.

CHAPTER 12

How We Will Create
a Vaikuṇṭha Planet

Wisdom from the Great leaders of
our Earth Planet

Kṛṣṇa, the Supreme Personality of Godhead, first spoke the Bhagavad-gita 140 million years ago to the sun-god, Vivasvan, from whom all the surya-vamsa, sun dynasty, ksatriyas kings descended down to the present time and Lord Rāmacandra was pleased to appear in the same surya-vamsa dynasty later in the Treta-yuga.

Later still, Lord Kṛṣṇa appeared in the candra-vamsa dynasty of ksatriyas, the lunar dynasty of great kings in Dvapara-yuga. All these kings were saintly, being headed as they were by the Supreme Personality of Godhead. It was only until much later that the kings became polluted and contaminated in the form of Dhrtarastra and Duryodhana.

2,600 years ago, Lord Buddha accepted the patronage of King Asoka and was thus able to spread His philosophy of *ahimsa paro dharmo*, non-violence to all living entities, as the supreme religion, throughout the Eastern world.

Although Lord Caitanya Mahaprabhu completely shunned pounds-shillings and pence men 500 years ago, He did accept into His fold great rulers like King Prataparudra, Rāmananda Raya, and the Chand Kazi. Jiva Gosvami accepted King Akhbara, the Great, as his disciple, and Narottama Dāsa Thakura raised a whole village of 4,000 people to Krsna consciousness in one go.

Srila Bhaktisiddhanta Sarasvati Thakura was pleased to instruct the King of Tripura & Assam and accept his patronage in the late 19th century. Our own Srila Prabhupada was pleased to present his Srimad-Bhagavatam books to

the Prime Minister of India, Lal Badhura Sas-
tri, around 1962, and meet, and talk with Prime
Minister Indira Gandhi, as did Yamuna Devi
Dasi, Guru Dāsa, Bhanu Dāsa, Giriraja Dāsa
and Gopala Dāsa. The devotees met Prime
Minister Indira Gandhi on three separate occasions on and around 7th November 1970. Srila
Prabhupada met Prime Minister Indira Gandhi
a little later.

Sri Caitanya Mahaprabhu predicted His holy
name would be heard in every town, village
and city of the world and the world's leaders
can help us do that. Srila Prabhupada also took
the time to speak to the World Health Organization leader in Geneva in 1974.

Gopala Krsna Maharaja met with Indian
Prime Minister Atal Behari Bajpai, when he
attended the opening ceremony of the Iskcon
Delhi temple in 1996 and Gopala Krsna Maharaja also met Indian President Pratibha Patil in
Moscow, Russia. Also as a follow-up, Maha-
mantra Dāsa has been in touch with the Indian
Prime Minister's office a number of times over
the years, as has Devaki-nandana Dāsa. Jayapa-
taka Maharaja received an award from the King
of Nepal. Bhakti Tirtha Swami and Krsna Dāsa

Swami were in touch with South Africa's President Nelson Mandela. The temple president, Kalamansara Dāsa received the Prime Minister of New Zealand in the Auckland Temple for 2 hours, who then, later offered to fund our Food for Life program there.

The Prime Minister of Macedonia came to Indradyumna Swami's lecture in Macedonia. Sivarāma Swami received a Gold Cross Medal from the President of Hungary and the latter gave the devotees a building which they have converted into a college-temple.

Radhanatha Swami has met President Obama of the USA, who recalls eating out at a Hare Kṛṣṇa restaurant in Hawaii, as a student. Gauri Dāsa and Sruti-dharma Dāsa have met British Prime Minister Tony Blair, Gordon Brown (dubbed Govardhana Brown), David Cameron, Theresa May and Boris Johnson on a few occasions at No. 10 Downing Street, where Dipavali is celebrated every year now. Navin Kṛṣṇa Dāsa has received Queen Elizabeth II and the Duke of Edinburgh at the Kṛṣṇa Avanti School in Harrow, and met with David Cameron on a few occasions. The British Government is looking to invest in 24

Kṛṣṇa Avanti Schools in the UK. Sutapa Dāsa has talked to Queen Elizabeth and Jayadeva Dāsa has met with British Prime Minister Tony Blair.

In September 1999, when I was temple president, I met with Indian Prime Minister Atal Behari Bajpai, in his constituency, Lucknow, U.P., India at Raja Bhavan and invited him to come to Lucknow's first Sri Jagannatha Rathayatra at the time, and also to help build a temple in Lucknow. Srila Bhaktivinoda Thakura predicted the catalyst for Kṛṣṇa consciousness globally, would start from the then Prussia, modern day Lithuania, Estonia, Latvia, and parts of Germany and Russia. Our first country would be Mauritius, but first we must take India, before the whole world really embraces Kṛṣṇa.

Srila Prabhupada has his 18-day plan to take over the whole world. Prime Minister Narendra Modi has introduced cow protection, directed the cleaning-up of the Ganga and Yamuna and on the world stage introduced International World Yoga Day, 21st June, to be celebrated every year. Indian President Pranava Mukherjee has attended the foundation ceremony for the Sri Caitanya Mahaprabhu Museum in Calcutta and directed funds towards it.

In Holland the Government has allocated land for the devotees to build a college-temple under the European Union. Indian President Sankara Dayal had received the Bhagavad-gita from HH B.S. Parivrajaka Maharaja and B.S.Sannyasi Maharaja. Bhakti-Caru Swami has spoken at the United Nations. Kirtiraja Dāsa and Drumila Dāsa have distributed books to many leaders of society. Following on from all these events and activities, Uttama-sloka Dāsa has set-up S.U.N., the Spiritual United Nations, an NGO affiliated to the UN and I am now looking to meet Secretary-General of the United Nations, Ban Ki-moon, in London at Central Hall, Westminster on 14th October 2015 to discuss how best we can create a Vaikuṇṭha planet out of this Earth planet, before he leaves office on 31st December 2016 as the lasting legacy of his term in office.

What Does a Vaikuṇṭha Planet Look Like?

❖ *No anxiety for all 8 billion people.*

❖ *There is one Emperor for the whole world*

❖ *guided by a brahmanical council of pure sages.*

❖ *Society is divided up into 4 divisions, namely*

❑ *The intellectual class of people, like the spiritual leaders, priests, academics, and teachers.*

❑ *The administrative class of people, namely, the politicians, the military, the police, and those meant to keep the peace and law and order, to protect the other physically less able sections of society.*

❑ *The food-producing class, that is, the farmers, the industrialists, the business class and the cow protectors.*

❑ *And finally, those who would like to work for the other divisions of society, the artisans, the entertainers, and workers of all description.*

❖ *There will be one book for everyone, namely, Bhagavad-gita As It Is, one God, namely, Lord Sri Kṛṣṇa, one mantra: Hare Kṛṣṇa, Hare Kṛṣṇa, Kṛṣṇa Kṛṣṇa, Hare Hare / Hare Rāma, Hare Rāma, Rāma Rāma, Hare Hare, and one work, service to the Supreme Personality of Godhead, Kṛṣṇa.*

❖ *People in general will be taught four languages, namely, samskrta, bengali, english and their mother tongue.*

❖ *There will be peace and prosperity across the whole globe and there will be full employment everywhere for everyone.*

❖ *The gold standard will predominate and there will be no artificial currency.*

❖ *Everyone will fast from grains twice a month and all the standard religious festivals will be celebrated by everyone.*

❖ *The four regulative principles will be adhered to by all the higher classes,namely:-*

❑ *no meat, fish or eggs*

❑ *no gambling*

❑ *no intoxication*

❑ *no illicit sex*

❑ *no cows, bulls, calves or buffalos will be killed for any reason.*

❖ *There will be no starvation, wars, pestilence, famine or disease and everyone in general will live for as long as they wish, going back to Godhead at the end of their life.*

❖ *The British Empire of Kṛṣṇa consciousness will reign and people will live simply and think highly.*

❖ *Everyone will be taught how to grow their own food and everyone will be self-sufficient, self-sustained, and self-realized.*

❖ *Everyone will have access to the Emperor, after going through the right channels and there will be justice for all.*

❖ *Everyone will have access to all the books of His Divine Grace A. C. Bhaktivedanta Swami Srila Prabhupada for more detailed information on how to lead their lives.*

❖ *This will be the blueprint for the planet for the next 9,467 years and everyone will recognise and worship Lord Sri Kṛṣṇa Caitanya Mahaprabhu as the yuga-avatara for this day and age.*

CHAPTER 13

A Message to Ban Ki-Moon, UN Security-General

The missing link in international political affairs is God. We want peace without God. That is not possible. All our plans for peace for the last 70 years are slowly crumbling because we have forgotten the most essential ingredient in all our dealings and that is God.

Unless we have a clear conception of the Absolute Truth all our hopes for peace are a completely useless waste of time. We see that as individuals, as families, as communities, as individual nation states and collectively, as a United Nations body as a whole. Without a full and proper understanding of the Supreme

Personality of Godhead, all our plans for peace will ultimately lead to defeat.

Religion is not the cause of war.
Man's misunderstanding of religion
is the cause of war.

True religion unites the people. Fanaticism divides the people. So, a proper understanding of religion and its rightful place in an individual's life, in the life of a nation and in the life of the planet as a whole is inextricably linked to who is God, who am I, what is my relationship with Him, how am I to act based on that relationship, and ultimately how can I develop my love for that person – this is the most crucial aspect of all human affairs on the planet.

Without an understanding of this based on authoritative sources, we are simply skirting around the problem and so are doomed to fail, time again. The United Nations Charter and its people are desperately seeking a solution to all its myriad of problems, and it is as though we are blowing on a boil to cure it. We must face the problem head-on and lance it, if are to solve it at its very root. Unless we seek the right authority on how to get help, we will fall short of a complete solution. We must approach the right person to help us and then everything will come out well. That person is God or His true representative.

My First Meeting with Ban Ki-moon, Secretary-General of the United Nations

On Friday 5th February 2016, Caturbhuja Prabhu and I went to see Ban Ki-moon, the Secretary-General of the United Nations, in Central Hall, Westminster, London, in precisely, the same place where the first United Nations meeting was held in October 1945, some 70 years ago, by the founding fathers of the United Nations. We left home from 101, Marley Walk, Willesden Green, NW2 4PY at 08.45am and walked to the top of the road, running to catch the No. 266 bus to Willesden Library, then a 52 bus to Vauxhall Bridge Road, Victoria, then another bus to Parliament Square to get to Central Hall, Westminster just before 10.30am, after all the buses waded through long traffic jams a lot of the way.

Caturbhuja Prabhu made all the necessary clearance checks for admittance and entrance to the main hall where Baroness Anelay was just finishing giving her speech to about 1500 people, many of whom were ambassadors and diplomats from their own countries, followed by Sir Jeremy Greenstock, who was just about to introduce His Excellency Ban Ki-moon, Secretary-General of the United Nations to the packed audience. In broken muffled English, Ban Ki-moon spoke for one hour and took questions afterwards. A few of the things he said were:-

❖ *125 million people are starving at the present time, that is, if they were all in one country it would be the 11ᵗʰ largest country in the world after Japan.*

❖ *Heads of state should stop keep coming up to me for their national interests, and think globally in the interests of everyone on the planet.*

❖ *If you put women on the board of your directors, you will make more profits, Forbes 500 companies survey found.*

❖ *99% of the world's wealth is owned by 1% of the world's population, actually by just 62 people. Distribute your wealth.*

❖ *We, in the UK, have absolutely no idea of what is going in the world outside. I feel psychologically damaged every time I visit some of these countries. A one day trip there takes me 20 days to recover.*

❖ *For the first time ever, 150 Heads of state spontaneously got together in one day, the other day.*

❖ *We collected $10 billion in one day yesterday for Syria, in London. This is totally unprecedented.*

❖ *The UK is to be commended for its international charitable giving.*

After the speech, Sir Jeremy wound up the proceedings and Caturbhuja and I (at about 12 noon) walked out the main hall to see if we could distribute my pocket-size Bhagavad-gita to Ban Ki-moon personally. A lady from Chatham House said she would pass it onto the organizers to give to Ban Ki-moon, but after I gave her the book I was not very satisfied that

Ban Ki-moon would actually get the book and read it.

So I went in search of Caturbhuja again and when I met him, he said, 'There will be another opportunity to see Ban Ki-moon at close quarters very shortly and you can give him your other Bhagavad-gita then.' So we all filed out and went downstairs to a much smaller room, and before I knew it, by Kṛṣṇa's mercy, I was face-to-face with Ban Ki-moon himself and shaking his hand a few times and then I offered him my Bhagavad-gita and he took it and said he would read it. I said, 'Please read the page where I have put the marker Chapter 5 verse 29 - the peace formula.' And then he passed the book to his security guards, who by now wanted to move me along, but I stood my ground and said I want to ask Ban Ki-moon a question, 'How can I become a spiritual advisor to the United Nations?' Ban said, 'What field do you want to advise in?' I said, 'Spirituality'. (I think he may not have heard me say 'spiritual' when I said 'spiritual advisor' the first time.) He said, 'There isn't a field for that yet.' I said, 'We ought to have one now, don't you think?' And I left it at that.

Man Mohan Gupta

Lord Kṛṣṇa's 3-step peace formula in
Bhagavad-gita Chapter 5 Text 29 is:

bhoktaram yajna-tapasam
sarva-loka-mahesvaram
suhrdam sarva-bhutanam
jnatva mam santim rcchati

This means if God is the creator of this whole material manifestation, then, logically, He must be its supreme proprietor or the owner of it, not us minute living entities, and then again if God has created this world, He would have done so for some reason, some purpose.

Here Kṛṣṇa explains that reason – for His unlimited pleasure. He is the supreme bhokta, the supreme enjoyer. Finally, Kṛṣṇa explains that He wishes to share His opulences with His kind and lovable living entities, as the supreme friend of all living entities.

So, as soon as we recognize God as, firstly, the supreme proprietor and secondly, as the supreme enjoyer of this world and thirdly, the supreme friend of all living entities, there is immediate peace in this world and no will want to encroach upon another's property or life. Few will deny that this is a practical peace formula.

Ban Ki-moon then made a short speech from the podium following on from a joke between Churchill, Roosevelt and Stalin and then it was announced that he would be moving to another room for his lunch.

So I followed the now much smaller group of people to the lunch room and sensing we would soon have to disperse I quickly caught the eye of the same bodyguard who was watching me before, and said to him, 'I want to create a Vaikuṇṭha planet out of this earth planet.

Can you help me, please?' He said,' what's a Vaikuṇṭha planet?' I said, 'It is a planet where 8 billion people can live without anxiety.' He said, '8 billion people without stress?' Shocked, but challenged, 'How are you going to that?' I said, 'By introducing International World Prayer Day'.

Man Mohan Gupta

*All 8 Billion people praying together.
A world that prays together, stays together.*

He smiled and in his broad New York accent said, 'Yes, you have the answer. I will personally like to come and join you. I am definitely going to tell Ban Ki-moon to do the same.

He will love your idea. Thank you.' I walked away parting smiles with him. I stayed a little longer till 1.30pm and then left Central Hall, accompanied with a little pitter-patter of drizzle whilst walking past Queen Elizabeth Conference Centre, St. Margaret's Church, Westminster Abbey, Parliament Square, The House of Commons, Big Ben and then Westminster Jubilee tube station, getting home by 2.00pm.

I took prasadam and then read Chapter 8 of the Bhagavad-gita before ringing the surgery for my liver test and spoke to Mukunda, Bhaja Hari's son, for Bhaja Hari Prabhu to ring me back, which he did and I told him, 'I just gave a copy of your Bhagavad-gita to Ban Ki-moon today.'

He said, 'Who's Ban Ki-moon?' I said,' The Secretary-General of the United Nations.' He said, 'That's big.' I said,' Please print 8 billion copies of your pocket-size Bhagavad-gita's with Devanagari text and full index, like Hamsa Dutta's copy, and I will pay you for them and distribute them myself.'

HariBol! Param vijayate sri Krsna samkirtanam!

Written by

Kāraṇodakaśāyī Viṣṇu Dāsa Adhikārī

on Friday 5th February 2016 and typed up on Saturday 6th February 2016 at 101, Marley Walk, Willesden Green, London, NW2 4PY, UK at 9.30pm.

My Meeting with Present Secretary-General of the United Nations, His Excellency Antonio Guterres at 9.30pm on Friday 3rd June 2016 at the Barbican Centre, London, United Kingdom

At the above time and place, I met the present Secretary-General of the United Nations, Antonio Guterres and offered him a copy of my pocket-size Bhagavad-gita As It Is, which he kindly received and said he would be happy to read it. I also mentioned to him that the Peace

Formula for the whole world is on page 264, Chapter 5 Text 29, please read it and implement it. He said he would.

My Meeting with Oxford Professors of Physics and Mathematics and other Science Luminaries at London's New Scientist Live Event at Excel on Friday 11th October 2109, Saturday 12th October 2019 and Sunday 13th October 2019

On Friday 11th October 2019, I first of all asked American space expert, Chuck Lauer of Spacebit, just what is the fascination with space? He was a little pressed to give any reasonable answer, so I suggested would it not therefore be better to spend our money closer to home, again he baulked at the question, but agreed the real problems are on the planet, not in space. I then went over to the Apollo missions site and asked two experts there, when was the last Apollo mission, they said 1972.

Jolly poor show, I thought. I then attended a talk given by Dr. David Gems of The Institute of Healthy Ageing at University College London on A Cure for Ageing and asked him

if he was aware of people who live in the Him-
alayas, who live very long lives there. He said
no he was not aware of them, as he could not
verify their age. I suggested that might be an
avenue to explore, possibly.

Printed in Poland
by Amazon Fulfillment
Poland Sp. z o.o., Wrocław